COMMUNISM

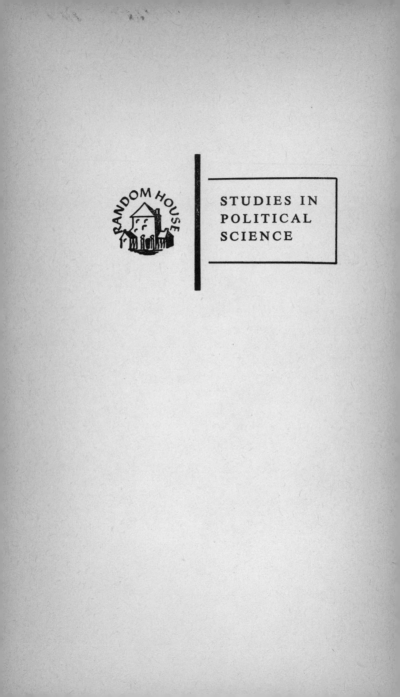

RANDOM HOUSE

STUDIES IN
POLITICAL
SCIENCE

COMMUNISM

Alfred G. Meyer

RANDOM HOUSE • NEW YORK

Contents

PREFACE

This introduction to communism in its various guises and functions is intended for a broad public of advanced and beginning students, policy-makers, and the proverbial intelligent layman—for anyone, in short, who wants to study the subject with a minimum of political passion. I stress my effort to achieve political detachment because I feel that much of what the general public reads about communism so caters to an attitude of disapproval that it can enlighten no one.

Some may feel that the essay style I have chosen does not suit the purposes of the book; but I believe that an author must reveal himself even when endeavoring to outline his subject and the principal controversies about it. I have tried to counteract personal interpretation by guiding the reader, at every major step, to the ample literature in this field.

I have profited from comments by Samuel Krislov, Archibald Singham, and Donald Urquidi, who read brief sections of the manuscript. Some of my statements would have been different or would not have been made prior to my 1958 trip to the USSR and Poland. For this enlightening travel I am grateful to the Inter-University Travel Grant Committee. To the administration of Michigan State University I owe thanks for releasing me from teaching for a quarter so that I could complete the manuscript. My special gratitude goes to Charles D. Lieber, of Random House, who encouraged me to write this Study, and to Mrs. Leonore C. Hauck, of the same firm.

ALFRED G. MEYER

I

Introduction

The word "communism" means different things to different people. To many political leaders in colonial nations, it implies revolt against the white man's rule, liberation from colonialism, and rapid industrialization, aided by Soviet money or advice. To French or Italian workers, it implies defense of lower-class interests and sympathy with Soviet foreign policy. Western intellectuals tend to regard it as a utopian ideal tarred by inhuman practices. To the policeman, it is an international conspiracy of power-mad criminals. To the Soviet citizen, the word connotes, in one sense, a meaningful goal his society is striving to attain within the foreseeable future and, in a broader sense, the entire Soviet way of life, with its rewards and its hardships. Communism means an ideal, a political movement, a method of analysis, and a way of life. It may even mean a set of attitudes which psychologists might be able to reduce to a syndrome of personality traits. Some people regard it as the product and property of Western civilization, while others see it primarily as an anti-Western revolt, or as a denial of all Western values and traditions.

Obviously, communism is protean; its meaning depends on time and place, circumstance, and on the point of view of the observer. Even its articulate ethos, Marxist theory, clothes itself in garbs of many hues. The theory itself distinguishes different levels of understanding and tries, accordingly, to speak to different publics.[1] It also views reality on different levels of concreteness or abstraction, so that it takes long-, short-, and intermediate-range views of the setting, the goals, and the strategies of the communist movement. Outsiders, meanwhile, note the tendency toward the development of an esoteric communist language which, some maintain, serves as a complicated code only the initiates know how to decipher.[2]

Because the present study is to serve as a general introduction to the subject, I am obliged to approach it eclectically, as perhaps any political phenomenon ought to be approached, if adequate understanding is to be gained. In viewing communism in its various aspects, we shall pay particular attention to a number of problems that run through these various facets of our subject: The element of change—what transformations have communist ideas and practices undergone from the time of Marx to the time of Mao? The element of diversity—what different schools of communism have arisen and which have survived? How important are the differences between communism in France and communism in Malaya, between communist revolutionaries and communist government officials? Is it meaningful to call these various political forces by the same name? Finally, we shall try to assess the nature of the much-discussed "challenge" of communism. Should communism be regarded as a threat to Western civilization, and, if so, in what way is it a threat? Is communism likely to gain adherents and make converts in the years and decades to come? If so, what makes it attractive; what elements in it appeal to people not yet committed to it?

My main emphasis will be on the theory of communism; and perhaps this requires justification, because many scholars would dismiss communist theory as irrelevant. They would describe communist doctrine as a grab bag of ideas cynically used by Machiavellian manipulators at the head of communist governments and parties to justify whatever policies they choose to adopt while seeking to gain or maintain power for its own sake. I do not agree with those writers who would derive all Soviet actions and institutions from Marxist ideology. But neither is it entirely true, as many other scholars claim, that the "means have eaten up the ends." Although communism gives a great deal of emphasis to the final goal in its theories, its short-range planning and actions seem to be guided by the revisionist principle that the end is nothing, the means everything. Yet these means were derived from the ends. As Richard Lowenthal correctly says in a recent symposium on this problem, there can be no *Realpolitik* without ideological preconceptions.[3] The theory, moreover, is more than a set of goals. It is also a method of analysis, and it has remained a methodological gridwork through which its initiates view and explain reality. Finally, communism still is a definable state of mind; and the attitudes composing it are also derived in part from Marxism.

In short, communist theory is more than rationalization. Undoubtedly, the thoughts and actions of communist leaders are determined in significant measure by the intellectual heritage of Marx, Lenin, and Stalin. But even if this were not so, the fact remains that their ideology remains one of the strongest forces active in the world today. And therefore it must be studied by anyone trying to understand contemporary history.

However, we cannot hope to understand the strength—and the weaknesses—of communist ideas without examining communism as a system of government, a way of life, and an active political movement. Nor can we hope to grasp the meaning of communist ideas without studying the historical and political context within which they were shaped and changed. We shall therefore have to discuss the various phases of Soviet rule, which are as different from each other as present-day Soviet Russia is from present-day America or even from present-day China, and also the various phases of the policies of the international communist movement.

The resulting image will be complex and, for those who like easy generalizations, unsatisfactory. In order to provide a framework for all the loose pieces we shall have in our hands—and at the risk of oversimplification—let me suggest one such generalization: it seems to me that twentieth-century communism, in all its variations, can be understood to some extent if we regard it as our age's equivalent to seventeenth-century puritanism (which includes as many varying phenomena as communism).* To support this suggestion, let me draw attention to some of the innumerable parallels that can be drawn between the two phenomena.

Puritanism and communism share a number of important broad ideas and political goals. Both claimed to strive for liberty and against tyranny, even though in the name of liberty both set up starkly autocratic regimes. Both claimed to fight for equality and human brotherhood and against the privileges or abuses of ruling classes and hierarchies; yet both set up societies marked by gross inequalities of reward, and in (thier) ideologies they found justification for such inequalities. Both claimed overriding justfication—be it God's will or historical inevitability—for destroying institutions they regarded as artificial, unnatural, or imposed. Both, finally, claimed that their aim was to carry out the ideals of revolutions that had preceded them by a century or more. The puritans gave themselves their name because their avowed aim was to fulfill, or purify, the Reformation; whereas communism promises to fulfill the broken promises of the French Revolution.

Puritanism as well as communism are theories of salvation and damnation, incorporating the notion of inevitability (predestination). Both movements fought (or fight) for an invincible cause, guided and strengthened by a

* Similarities can also be seen between communism and later forms of puritanism, for instance, Victorianism.

Holy Writ that played a central role in shaping the minds of entire generations. Both the puritans and the communists are fully convinced that "objective reality" or "God's will" can be known through careful study of the scriptures. Both movements developed their thought into complicated and involved systems of ideas that include theories of history, human nature, society, and the entire universe, and provide standards for behavior, including a theory of leadership and obedience. In both cases, moreover, the revolutionary zeal of the educated spokesmen appealed to broad strata of the lower, underprivileged classes, who were exhorted to despise and destroy the prevailing authorities; yet, once the leaders had installed themselves in power, that same zeal caused them to impose intolerable conditions and superhuman standards of performance on the citizens.

In both puritanism and communism we have, I think, cases of liberational movements gone sour and pessimistic, movements that therefore are marked by strange ambivalences in judgment and contradictions in both goals and methods. For both, an intellectual point of departure is the belief in the sovereignty of the autonomous human personality; in one case it is the individual in his direct relationship to his God, in the other case it is the proletariat in its crucial role in history. But in both cases serious doubt has arisen. For the puritans, this implied a renewed emphasis on original sin; for the communists beginning with Lenin, the belief that the working class by itself could never attain consciousness. In both movements, the practical consequence was that the earlier democratic conception that men would freely and spontaneously choose the road to (heavenly or earthly) salvation gave way to the idea that the elect, the vanguard, the chosen few would have to force the masses into salvation. Yet, while the individual (or the class) is regarded as weak and untrustworthy, while the movement has little faith in the autonomous personality, it still burdens the individual with grave responsibility for his actions and thoughts. Distrust in human nature or an emphasis on original sin is accompanied by the attempt to make every man into a fully rational being or into a saint, while the gloomy realization that this task might be impossible drives the movement to manipulation, coercion, and terror, carried out in both cases by an organization of the elect which coöpts its members, while going through the motions of elections or other democratic procedures. In organization, in procedure, in the purges they carried out, and in their actual and pretended relationship to government authorities (once a puritan or communist government has been created), the organization of the elect and the Communist Party bear striking resemblances to each other.

The underlying pessimism is expressed in the conviction that Satan (or capitalism) will surely defeat the cause of righteousness if the movement relents for but a little moment in its zealous devotion to the dogma, in its intolerance of deviation and laxness. Indeed, the devil lurks behind the most angelic masks, and both the puritan and the communist are therefore witch hunters, who tend to explain untoward developments by the weakest of all social theories—the conspiratorial theory. At the basis of the deep pessimism that characterizes both puritanism and communism is, perhaps, the fact that both these revolutionary movements were only partly successful, that they were forced to *coexist* with their enemy. Theoretically, neither movement was prepared for prolonged coexistence during which it might be obliged to have friendly or at least normal relations with the enemy. Both were profoundly disturbed by the experience.

Coexistence fortified the tendency of both puritans and communists to see everything in black and white and to divide mankind into friends and enemies, recognizing no shadings or positions in between truth and falsehood. Both are totalitarian in that they seek to infuse every realm of human endeavor with the spirit of their movement. Everything a man may do has religious (or political) significance. No pursuits are undertaken for their

own sake, but must be given the spirit of *partiinost*.*
Precisely because the movements are forced to accommodate "temporarily" to coexistence with the foe, they
must banish all thoughts of lasting or meaningful accommodation. Because of this pessimism and the resulting ambivalence, the urge to cleanse out what is rotten and
wrong is given a note of frantic urgency. Every action
counts. Everything that is done is decisive.

Despite the otherworldly orientation of the puritans
and the lofty humanism of communist doctrine, both
movements must be characterized as intensely materialis-
tic and secular. The principal orientation of both can be
said to be *accumulation,* that is, economic growth. And
just as the American puritans went forth into the wilder-
ness to carry civilization to the aborigines, so communism
is the pioneer movement which in our century seeks to
civilize (in the material sense) the underdeveloped nations, which aims to bring social mobility and the spirit
of work to indolent cultures. There is about both movements the same missionary spirit, the same desire to
liberate all mankind from evil and sloth.

In both cases, finally, this mission is carried out with
an almost inhuman earnestness, with a complete lack of
a sense of humor, and a stern intolerance of frivolous-
ness and hedonism. The drabness of Soviet towns, the
stark utilitarianism of Chinese communist garments, the
primness of Soviet sex morality are as puritan as they
could be and remind us vividly of the pictures we have
seen of America in the days of her Western pioneers.
In both cases, the individual is to be serious, thrifty, and
single-minded in his devotion to the goal of accumulating
wealth.

The similarities I have pointed out have been noticed
by previous observers.[4] But they deserve mention nevertheless because I think that the comparison gives us a
rather unusual view of communism, an angle of vision
that might help to explain features and relationships

* For an explanation of this term, see p. 121.

which might otherwise remain puzzles. In addition, I must confess that I find the *déjà-vu* feeling this perspective gives me a bit reassuring; for the comparison suggests that communism might not be as novel, as strange, or as alien to Western traditions as it appears to most of us, and as many of its adherents would like to make it seem. At the same time, as a decidedly anti-puritan person, I find that this view adds support to the antipathy I feel toward various features in the development of communism, even though it does help to explain them.

Let us then analyze the growth, the ideas, and the way of life of this twentieth-century puritanism, beginning with its own Good Book, the writings of Karl Marx and Friedrich Engels.

2

Marxist Theory

The emergence of nineteenth-century industrial society brought massive social dislocation and misery. Technological progress made entire classes of small producers and distributors obsolete, impoverished them, degraded them in the social scale, and forced them into the burgeoning cities, where unspeakable working and living conditions awaited them. Socialism as a mass movement began as the rebellion of the working class against their misery. Sporadic, almost aimless uprisings, such as those of the weavers in Silesia, the machine-wrecking Luddites in England, or the numerous working-class rebellions of 1848, mark the beginnings of the socialist movement. As a political theory, it developed when the workers' lot was contrasted with the liberal rhetoric prevailing at the time. Its point of departure was the assertion that the ideals of the American and French revolutions—liberty, equality, brotherhood, and the right to a human existence—had been betrayed; and that the promise of these revolutions could be fulfilled only if political rights were matched by social

and economic equality, by wiping out the difference between rich and poor. Beyond this, we cannot generalize
about advocates or theorists of socialism. They have dif-
fered sharply not only over the definition of the kind of
society that would rectify these ills but even more over the
methods that would bring it into existence. They have
included atheists and believers, pacifists and terrorists,
criminals and saints, authoritarians and anarchists, and all
shadings in between. The variety of socialist schools that
has developed in the last 165 years is made clear to us
when we realize that, in the vague sense I have given to
the word, almost everyone today is a socialist or has accepted socialist ideals.[1]

Communism regards itself as the legitimate heir of all
that is valid and good in the socialist tradition. It looks
upon the working-class revolts of the early nineteenth
century as the beginnings of its own movement and regards the first socialists, beginning with Gracchus Babeuf,
as precursors of its most honored prophets, Marx and
Engels (who, incidentally, preferred to call themselves
communists rather than socialists, in order to emphasize
their disagreements with other socialists).

The precursors of Marx and Engels are often referred
to as "utopian socialists." This term was used by the
Marxists themselves in criticism of both the detailed descriptions of the coming socialist society which earlier theorists had given and their failure to indicate how these
societies might be brought into existence.[2] In contrast,
Marx and Engels regarded their communism as scientific
socialism. They claimed to have proven that the coming
of socialism was inevitable; and their entire doctrine is an
attempt to support this assertion. Marxism can therefore
be defined as that school of socialism which seeks to
prove that socialism is inevitable.

As we shall see a little later, Marxists support this assertion partly by moral argument: capitalism so degrades the
individual, so frustrates his potentialities for creative development, that life under it is hell on earth, a mockery
of all the ethical commands associated with the Christian-

Liberal tradition. But man still retains his innate ability to shape a good life for himself, through socialism.

Marx and Engels, however, denied that they were moral philosophers or prophets preaching reform to an evil society. When they asserted the inevitability of socialism, they used the word "inevitable" in a descriptive (or, as they would have put it, scientific) sense. The existing system, they thought, simply could not last, and all the conditions necessary for the birth of socialism had come into being. The core of this doctrine was and remains the Marxist description of capitalism and the "laws" governing it—that is, the manner in which the system functioned. According to these laws, capitalism was well suited to ensure economic growth in the early industrial age; and Marx therefore assigns the most important place to capitalism among the stages in the march of human progress. No social philosopher, perhaps, has rivaled the songs of praise that Marx and Engels sang to capitalism in their *Communist Manifesto*. At the same time, however, Marxism asserts that the same laws that made capitalism advance the progress of mankind would bring misery, chaos, crisis, and final breakdown to the mature capitalist society. Institutions, habits, and intellectual traditions that had once strengthened the system would burden and fetter it intolerably and would hasten its collapse.

The fundamental law governing the Marxist model of capitalism is that of the market. In basing his analysis on this law, Marx follows in the footsteps of Adam Smith and other "classical" economists. He differs from them on several counts. For one thing, he places market economies into historical perspective by pointing out that they were preceded by different systems. There are societies in which men produce only to satisfy their immediate needs or those of their masters. Under capitalism, however, they produce marketable commodities; and all their economic activity is guided, even dictated, by the market. Another assertion distinguishing Marxism from classical economic theories is that under capitalism the labor power of the "immediate producers"—the workers—is bought and sold

as if it were a commodity. Therefore, the very lives of
people who are compelled to work for a living are subject
to the laws of the market. Life has become a market
place, with human work, human emotions, human spirit
bought and sold as a commodity.

To Marx, this transformation of human labor power
into a commodity is the specific feature which distinguishes capitalism from all other market economies and
therefore from all other modes of production as well.
Since, according to Marx, human labor is the only creative force, its subjection to the laws of the market intro-
duced into that market a curious element both constructive and disruptive: a commodity which, through the
creation of values, could not only reproduce itself but
could create far more than its own market value.

Before we pursue this, we must note one other line of
argument connected with the definition of capitalism as
that mode of production in which human labor power
has become a commodity. I have in mind the attempt
Marx and Engels made to show beyond any doubt that
capitalism was an exploitative system. To do so, they
again followed in the footsteps of classical economics by
incorporating in their market theory a theory of value.
Most Western economists today do not take the Marxist
theory of value seriously and tend to regard the very
notion of value as meaningless. They have usually failed
to see, however, the crucial role which the Marxist theory
of value plays, not as a concept in economic analysis, but
as a description of *social* relationships in a market economy; and of particular significance here is the relationship
between capitalist and worker, because, on the basis of
his particular definition of value and the classical laws of
the market, Marx could argue that the workers, selling
their labor power at its true value, were nevertheless
cheated out of a portion of what their labor produced.

From the concept of human labor as a commodity producing surplus value and from the relationship of this
human commodity to the "dead" commodities (materials,
machines, and so forth) used in production, Marx derived

additional laws governing both the growth and collapse of capitalism. These laws describe capitalism as a system compelled by its inner dynamic to accumulate capital at an ever-increasing rate and to invest it in new enterprises even though a constantly falling rate of profit made investment more and more difficult. The force of these laws was further seen to drive increasing numbers of capitalists to their ruin, swelling the ranks of the propertyless proletariat. Fiercely competing with each other, the workers would drive down the market value of human labor power, creating additional misery for the proletariat. Capitalism was therefore a system that had, through technological and social progress, led mankind to the threshold of an era in which the material needs of all humanity could be filled, if only the technological achievements could be used rationally. But the laws governing capitalist production had caused the system to become entangled in hopeless difficulties: a free-enterprise system in which all individuals operated blindly and helplessly; a productive capacity that could not be used; surplus human beings who could not be employed; surplus commodities that could not be sold nor given away, even while poverty was increasing. These and similar problems, Marx and Engels believed, capitalism could not possibly solve without destroying itself. Inevitably, therefore, the system would collapse, and socialism would rise from the ruins. This death and rebirth of society would take the form of a revolution in which the proletariat would expropriate the capitalists and reorganize the economy on completely different, and rational, principles. Society would then be able to satisfy all men's material needs. Inequality and exploitation would be abolished. Oppressive institutions and inhuman behavior would become superfluous and dysfunctional and would wither away. As a matter of fact, all institutions, habits, traditions, beliefs, behavior patterns, and the like, now confining and constraining human beings and preventing them from freely being themselves, would become superfluous. For, having become fully rational, all men would also become convinced that their own private interests could be satisfied only if they were identified with the interests of all. Men would become like brothers. Their relations with each other would be free and easy and spontaneous. This belief in the coming brotherhood of men led many communists in the years immediately following the Russian revolution to believe that law courts and the police, money and wages, sexual morals and the institution of the monogamous family, and many other elements of social life would disappear in the very near future.

Crucial to this vision of inevitability was the belief that the proletariat would be equipped to destroy the old and erect the new. And, in Marxist theory, the working class is indeed endowed with education, rationality, discipline, organization, and other qualities which, taken together, transform them into a Chosen People who will lead mankind into an earthly Promised Land.

This image of the proletariat and the society within which it exists is based upon several important assumptions. There is, first, Marx's insistence that social studies are a science. To use his and Hegel's terminology: History proceeds in accordance with laws, *gesetzmässig,* and because of this it can be understood by men. This belief in man's ability to understand history is based, in turn, on the axiom that man is rational and therefore potentially free, freedom being defined as the ability to shape one's destiny and to develop one's inherent potentialities to the fullest extent.

The question that arises at once is one which Rousseau asked in the first page of his *Social Contract*: If man is free, why is he everywhere in chains? In the same spirit, Marx might have asked why man's fate is not freely made by him but is determined by his environment, even though man is rational. Rousseau's answer is that civilization corrupted and enslaved man. Marx's reply is rather similar. In his theory, man is the animal that *produces*—which means that man strives intelligently and purposively to master the forces and resources of nature. Except on the most primitive level, however, production is an organized activity, not of individuals, but of societies, which in conformity with their technological and scientific achievements develop social structures and institutions as a framework or machinery for carrying out the activity of production. For Marx, the history of mankind is the development of different modes of production, that is, of different types of social structures, from primitive and inefficient to highly complex and efficient ones, all of which must be seen primarily as machineries designed to master the forces of nature and to ensure man's survival and comfort.

The most important principle of social structuring, in Marx's theory, is the class structure. Marxism maintains that the division of labor in all societies has led to the development of classes, the different classes being defined by their relations to the essential means of production. And, since control over these means of production confers decisive power over the entire community, the class that wields such control is not only playing a different role in the economy, it also plays a different political role by becoming the ruling class.[8]

Marxism contains a theory of lag: although a correspondence can be traced between class structure and technology and general mode of production, these "forces of production" are seen as developing on and on while the "production relations" show tendencies toward becoming rigid and self-perpetuating. Human progress is conceived as proceeding at varying speeds. New forces of production win over older, and "lower," forces. A new ruling class controlling these new forces establishes itself and builds social institutions corresponding to the new mode of production. Once in power, however, the new ruling class seeks to perpetuate its rule even if it is made obsolete and superfluous by further economic progress. The class structure becomes a drag on further progress. The superstructure of institutions, ideologies, and habits, which once was part of the forces of progress, now paralyzes further development. The forces and relations of production are in conflict with each other. Man's past

actions dominate the present generation. They do so all
the more easily because men, according to Marx, are not,
as a rule, aware of their state of subjection to the forces
of the past. They believe they are masters of their fate
even while they have only a false consciousness of the
relationships that constitute the mainspring of their re-
spective societies. This false consciousness, which Marx
called ideology, enables men to live in unjust and moribund societies. But it also prevents them from seeing the
impending doom of these societies.

Thus man's freedom is only potential. But Marx believed that it could be realized. All his doctrine is based
on a yearning for freedom and on the assumption that
history is continual progress in the realization of freedom,
a movement toward a society worthy of man. This vision
of progress is related to a humanist ethic based on the
principle that "man, for man, is the highest being," and
that therefore everything which pains or degrades him
must be abolished. Like all socialists, Marx denounced the
free-enterprise system for having betrayed liberal values.
Unlike some of them, however, he went further and criticized *all* societies, past and present, for having betrayed
basic human values. His doctrine calls for the most radical
criticism of social institutions. Just as Rousseau and the
romantics had contended that civilization is evil and spoils
human nature, so Marx held that human relationships in
civilized society—torn as it is by class conflict—are false,
evil, unworthy; and that, in such a society, man is *alienated* from nature, his fellow man, and even himself. Class
societies dehumanize man. Marx's moral indignation at
such alienation pervades all his writings, even those that
preceded his economic analysis of capitalism. He was a
radical humanist before he became a Marxist.

In contrast, however, to present-day critics of mass culture and the bureaucratic society, Marx was an optimist.
As a matter of fact, his doctrine is the last example of the
great optimistic ideologies that have succeeded each
other in the Western tradition; it is, in that sense, the
direct heir of liberalism.[4]

This optimism is based on the idea that mankind can solve all its problems without divine assistance, because of man's essentially rational nature. Marx's view of human nature is Promethean; Marx sees man as capable, like Prometheus, of defying the gods and stealing their fire to provide himself with the warmth of material comfort and the light of knowledge. Marxism is an arrogant ideology, and religious thinkers in our day often condemn it as a "secular religion." In their view man is afflicted with original sin and therefore forever unable to solve all his problems. They regard the intention to create the good life on this earth as presumptuous and blasphemous, and they point out that the attempt to carry out this intention, condemned in advance to failure, must lead to totalitarian tyranny.*

Marx and Engels, however, had no such fears. To be sure, they foresaw and even welcomed a period of violence and dictatorship that would link capitalism with communism. Meaningful change, in their eyes, could not but take the form of revolution. No ruling class, they thought, had ever given up or would ever give up their power without a desperate struggle. Nor could the change from one mode of production to another proceed without the old superstructure of institutions and beliefs being smashed. History, they held, progresses in leaps; where certain features lag behind the development of the means of production, there must be sharp breaks with the past and a thorough overhauling of the social system, through terror and violence. They condoned this violence because it would be coercion of the few by the many, of the exploiters by the exploited, of the ruling class by the people. They also implied that the period during which this dictatorship of the working class would prevail would be brief. Finally, whatever dictatorial or totalitarian fea-

* Assuming that in fact secular religion tends to impose dictatorship on the people in its attempt to create an earthly paradise, we must be aware at the same time that heavenly religion, by postponing paradise to the hereafter, falls into the danger of being indifferent to human misery which could be alleviated by rational action.

tures the dictatorship of the proletariat would entail, Marx and Engels regarded it as but the transition to the Good Society, an inevitable albeit regrettable means to a moral end.

We must ask ourselves on what facts or presuppositions Marx and Engels based this glowing optimism. Was it not in conflict with their ambivalent appraisal of civilization, that is, with their belief that the material progress of mankind had led to the increasing dehumanization of man? To be sure, if man's alienation is a consequence of the division of labor, the class struggle, and the unequal distribution of the means of production, then it follows that alienation might be cured once private property and the class struggle have been abolished. If it is correct to trace the growth of oppressive institutions and deceptive ideologies to the special needs of class-torn societies, then surely it follows that tyranny, exploitation, and superstition are likely to wither away once the class struggle is a feature of the past. Even within the terms of Marxist ideas, however, it is by no means obvious why the revolution leading to such a classless society should ever occur; or why, if indeed the working class seizes power, it will know what to do with it to ensure that leap into the realm of freedom which Marx and Engels foresaw. On the contrary, if they were right in saying that man is dehumanized under capitalism and that the worker has been transformed into a commodity, a marketable piece of equipment, how could they impute to these same workingmen that rationality which would make the coming of socialism inevitable?

The answer is that, according to Marxist theory, the proletariat is so absolutely alienated that the mechanism by which the ruling classes have usually managed to divert the attention and stultify the minds of the exploited no longer functions. The worker under capitalism has been estranged so relentlessly from what sociologists today call primary organizations and loyalties that his consciousness can free itself from deceptive ideologies. Having been dehumanized, the worker becomes aware of his dehuman-

ization and understands the social system that has produced him. When men become conscious of themselves
as commodities, they will feel the urge to abolish that
mode of production which makes them commodities.
They will also have the power to do so. Marx and Engels
attributed to the working class not only full rationality
(born out of unprecedented misery) but also a number
of qualities that would enable them to be successful in
their striving to abolish capitalism. For one thing, the
proletariat in the period of mature capitalism would
constitute the overwhelming majority of the population.
Moreover, they would be well organized, having learned
the virtues of cooperation in the capitalist machine shop,
where work proceeded in cooperative fashion. By draft-
ing them into their armies, the ruling classes had also
trained the proletariat for warfare, and by educating them
in at least an elementary way had further equipped them
for the coming role as revolutionaries and rulers. Finally,
Marx and Engels assumed that as the class which by its
physical labor with modern machines was the only really
productive class in capitalist society, the proletariat was
also well prepared to expropriate the means of production
and assume command over them.

This image of the working class as combining rationality with power and therefore inevitably bound to lead
mankind into the Promised Land is a bold attempt to rec-
oncile the gloomy theory of alienation with the Promethean image of man. It must be regarded as the corner-
stone of Marxist theory.[5]

We recognize in this image a variation of a dream that
is at least as old as Socrates. He believed that true good-
ness cannot be theoretical but must be expressed in
works: one cannot know virtue without practicing it.
Something akin to this belief is inherent in the Marxist
belief that the self-consciousness of the proletariat will
impel it to act. But Marx also shared the idea of Socrates'
pupil Plato that ideas remain ineffectual if they are not
backed by power. This insight into the problem of power
caused Plato to wish for a philosopher who was either

himself a king or whose advice was accepted by a king. In Marx the awareness of the problem of power led to the statement that ideas become effective only when they get hold of the masses. Neither philosophy nor action is effective by itself; they must work together. It is not enough, wrote Marx, that the idea strive toward realization; reality should also be receptive to the idea. And it is this coincidence of revolutionary thought with revolutionary action that Marx saw in the working-class movement on the eve of the Revolution of 1848.

The reader might miss a treatment of Marxist philosophy in this short sketch, especially since almost any other treatment of Marxism, be it by communists or by Western scholars, would begin with an outline of dialectical materialism. The reason I am omitting such an outline is that Marxism is a social theory, not a universal philosophy. Marx was interested in human relationships and social institutions; he dealt with nature only insofar as it was part of human society, and he had use for philosophy only to the extent that it was identical with scientific method. He held, moreover, that every realm of existence must be understood in terms of its own laws; hence he did not contend that the methods and insights he advanced in his social theories were applicable to biology, physics, or general philosophy. There is, in short, a decidedly positivistic strain in Marxism. And yet, neither Marx nor Engels could escape or deny the profound influence which Hegelian philosophy exerted on them, a philosophy which focused its sights on concepts of reason and freedom and had developed a highly esoteric combination of ontology and logic, called dialectics.* In negating these elements of Hegelian philosophy, Marx nonetheless retained and transformed it. In his view, moral philosophy was inadequate or meaningless if it did not coincide with, or even take the form of, revolutionary action designed to change

* For an Introduction to Hegel's philosophy, see C. J. Friedrich's Introduction to *The Philosophy of Hegel* (Modern Library); Herbert Marcuse, *Reason and Revolution: Hegel and The Rise of Social Theory;* Humanities, 1955; and Robert Tucker, *Philosophy and Myth in Karl Marx,* Cambridge University Press, 1961.

reality. He saw philosophy and politics, thought and action, science and moral postulates, as coalescing, as Plato had hoped they would fuse in the philosopher-king. And just as the Platonic utopia demands a philosopher-king, so the entire structure of Marxist ideas is held together by the belief that the proletariat does indeed represent the merger of theory and practice. This belief, in turn, is the keystone of that "materialist" (read: sociological) dialectics into which Marx transformed Hegel's philosophy of reason. However, moral philosophy which becomes incarnate in the revolutionary proletariat, and a dialectic of reason which is "stood on its feet" and then becomes the history of human institutions have turned into a denial of abstract philosophy. Any attempt to abstract a universal philosophy from Marxism is therefore a distortion, and I should be prepared to argue this even though Engels himself, in violation of all his own positivistic statements, was the first to attempt this distortion.[6]

3

European Marxism,
1848–1914

The evidence is not altogether conclusive, but the impression prevails that when Marx and Engels wrote the manifesto of the Communist Party in 1847, summarizing their views with marvelous conciseness, they were momentarily expecting the end of capitalism. They thought that their ideas were but the articulation of actual feelings, of the actual consciousness shared by vast masses of proletarians who were prepared for revolutionary action and were waiting only for some historic event or for action by the enlightened leadership to set events in motion. Marx and Engels knew, as many other politically conscious people in Europe knew, that a revolution was brewing. They thought it would be the revolution of the proletariat.[1]

In fact, however, the working class played a comparatively negligible role in most of the upheavals that shook Europe in 1848. Moreover, in the subsequent years and even decades, the development of the working-class movement gave Marx and Engels little encouragement to expect the proletariat to rally to the banner of their ideas. Working-class parties were slow in getting organized; and when they did, their leaders (and followers) were not necessarily committed to Marxist doctrines.

This failure of the 1848 revolution, and the seeming unwillingness of the masses to become fully conscious (in the Marxist sense of the term) led to soul searching on the part of the fathers of the doctrine and caused them to make adjustments in their thoughts concerning the nature of capitalism, the aims and morphology of the revolution, and the strategy to be employed by the proletariat. Explanations had to be found for the failure; contemporary political constellations had to be examined for this purpose; and, in both cases, Marx and Engels were forced to pay closer attention to concrete phenomena at odds with the more abstract grand design of their theoretical model. Recognition of precapitalist features still affecting current politics was not, of course, regarded as a refutation of the theory, but it did complicate the task of analysis, self-orientation, and evaluation. Similarly, instead of preparing for the final act of revolution, as Engels, particularly, had done with joyous alacrity in 1848, Marx and Engels now felt compelled to study and discuss strategies that might prepare the ground for revolution and lead toward it; and here again short-range plans were likely to come into conflict with long-range expectations. Or, at least, the strategy of Marxist politics was obliged to consider measures and attitudes that the original theory of revolution simply had not incorporated—alliances with other radical movements, foreign policy problems, the evaluation of constitutional democracy from the point of view of the proletariat, and so forth. Various ranges of strategy were developed, and different aims—minimal, maximal, and in between—were formulated. In retrospect, many of these changes appear drastic when compared to the dreams of 1848; and one scholar has dramatized the contrast by stating that after 1848 Marx "became what is nowadays called an ex-Communist." [2]

Yet these drastic changes did not imply any fundamental changes in the grand conception. Rather, they can be regarded as refinements, concretization, elaboration, and extension of the doctrine. The intense and ceaseless intellectual activity of research, writing, and debating in which Marx and Engels engaged to the end of their lives, without ever completing their major task of systematic exposition, was solidly founded on the ideas they had elaborated in common in the five years or so before 1848.

This unfinished job of elaboration and extension made Marxism more complex, ambiguous, and fragmentary, hence more subject to controversial discussion, misinterpretation, and vulgarization. There are, indeed, many scholars who claim that the process of misinterpretation and vulgarization was begun by Engels himself. They would point out that Engels' book against Dühring is filled with naïve and shallow passages that do violence to Marx's sophistication, and that his attempts to apply Marxist ideas to the realm of natural science is based on gross misunderstanding. Against this argument, we have indications that Marx approved of the anti-Dühring manuscript. Be that as it may, however, Marxism has certainly not always been well understood, even by its own most devoted followers. The first important school that misunderstood and misrepresented Marxism were the theoreticians of the European socialist movement in the generation preceding World War I, the spokesmen of the Second International. Even though many of them battled fiercely to defend the letter of what had already become the Marxist Holy Writ against any attempts to revise or criticize it, Marxism in their hands became something quite different from the ideas of its founder. They turned his revolutionary radicalism into a comparatively tame search for gradual reform; for his fighting spirit they substituted something akin to fatalism; and instead of the contempt he had for liberal democracy, his followers had an honest veneration for constitutional government. The subtlety of Marxist dialectics became the shallow determinism which non-Marxist scholars have always had an easy time refuting.[3]

These disciples also perverted Marx's ideas by extending them—as Engels had begun to do—from social science into natural science and general philosophy. Marxist dialectics, a complex set of heuristic devices that had served to make Marx sensitive to subtle and involved relationships, is far too esoteric in language and complicated in ideas to become the ideology of a broad political movement. Nor did it fit the scientific concepts and prejudices then dominant in the educated world. For these and other reasons, the conceptual tools of Marx were abstracted from their context and transformed into an utterly inadequate philosophy, called "dialectical materialism," that was a caricature of Marx's thinking. Finally, the notion of the unity of theory and practice, central to Marxist ideas, was almost totally forgotten. Marxists no longer understood the importance which Marx and Engels had attributed to proletarian consciousness in their theory of revolution; and the notion of class consciousness itself was given a very different meaning. We shall see that some of these misinterpretations have found their way also into contemporary communist thought, while others have been rejected.

In trying to explain this process of vulgarization, we have called attention to the fragmentary state and the complexity of Marxist thought, as well as to the intellectual preconceptions of the Victorian age. We might have added that the jargon of Hegelianism presented a formidable obstacle to the understanding of Marxist ideas. But the most important reason for the transformation was undoubtedly the changing nature of the working-class movement.

Marxism found a mass basis only in the last two decades of the nineteenth century. For only then did the growing labor movement in Continental Europe adopt Marxism as its guiding ideology. By that time, however, the proletariat was quite different from the one described in the *Communist Manifesto*. Far from being impoverished, it was beginning to obtain its share—however modest—of the material benefits being reaped by the business community in these decades. Moreover, whether because of the continued agitation for constitutional reform, or for whatever other reasons, the working class was given the franchise, formed political parties, and began to participate in constitutional politics.

Instead of being absolutely alienated, therefore, significant sections of the working class, and especially their political leaders and trade-union officials, began to feel themselves part of a functioning social system that only needed to be improved to be altogether acceptable. From revolutionists they turned into reformists and constitutional democrats. Abandoning the plan to smash the existing system, they began to strive for improvements in working and living conditions, and equal political rights. And in the end, when an international war forced them to decide between their loyalty to their class and their loyalty to their country, most of them, at least for the time being, abandoned internationalism and chose patriotism.

There was therefore a growing gap between the revolutionary theory and the reformist practice of the Marxist movement, which sooner or later would call for serious readjustments. Most of those who were aware of the discrepancy sought to revise Marxist ideas to bring them into line with current political strategies, although a handful of radical leaders tried in vain to revise the movement's political program to bring it back into line with revolutionary theory.* Those who did not see, or did not wish to see, the divergence of doctrine and practice were forced to align them by reinterpreting and misinterpreting Marxist thought. This process of reinterpretation gradually merged with that of revision; and both have gone on apace ever since the end of the last century. The result has been that democratic socialism has almost completely divorced itself from Marxist theories.

* Even these radicals, of course, were forced to make adjustments in the theory. We shall come back to these adjustments when we discuss the communist theory of imperialism.

4

Principles of Leninism

The gap between theory and practice was even wider in prerevolutionary Russia than in Russia after the revolution. The tsarist empire must be characterized as a relatively backward society, a term that is not meant to imply moral or cultural superiority of other nations, but denotes only one thing, technological inferiority and the resultant lower productivity. Nor does it imply that the country did not have its share of highly educated, cultured people who made important contributions to science, art, and philosophy. Russia before the revolution of 1917 was backward because in the nations of Western and Central Europe she faced neighbors who had more productive economies and therefore were also stronger militarily and politically.

Economically advanced nations are usually regarded by their less-fortunate neighbors as presenting a threat to themselves, and much of Russia's history can be explained in terms of reaction to the technological superiority of the West. The great dilemma faced by political leaders in

underdeveloped areas is this: What they regard as the
threat of economically advanced nations can be mitigated
only by adopting the technology which is at the basis of
the presumed threat. For a nation that wishes to maintain its established culture and traditional way of life, the
need to "westernize" is extremely painful. But the rulers
of old Russia were well aware of this need, and some of
Russia's tsars were nothing less than revolutionaries who
tried to transform radically the society over which they
ruled. To be sure, while they sought to introduce Western
technology, science, and administrative skills, they did not
wish to endanger their own rule. Consequently, their aim
was to westernize selectively; but in this they did not succeed. On the contrary, with Western technology and administration came Western progressive ideas and movements of reform.

Old Russia was ruled by emperors who claimed absolute power. Their arm of government was a civil and military bureaucracy, the officers of which were recruited
mainly from the landowning aristocracy, a privileged leisure class whose wealth was measured not only in land
but also in serfs. They had obtained their privileges as
compensation for services rendered to the tsars. But in
the eighteenth century they were freed of their service
obligation while retaining their privileges. Indeed, service
itself became a privilege of the nobility. After the nobles
were freed of their duties, the serfs remained in bondage
for about another hundred years. They were released only
in the second half of the nineteenth century. But the land
they were given at this time was so inadequate that they
remained in economic bondage to their old masters. Constantly on the brink of economic ruin and smarting under
legal discrimination, the Russian peasants, constituting
about nine-tenths of the population, were therefore a dissatisfied class and potential fomenters of revolution.[1]

Toward the end of the nineteenth century, industry
began to develop in Russia and a working class grew
which found itself laboring and living under very poor
conditions, thus forming another revolutionary class,

which was easy to organize and from the very beginning was conscious of its grievances. With the growth of industrialism, a middle class of merchants, capitalists, and well-educated professional people also arose. This class at once sought to participate in the political process and began to advance such aims as free enterprise and democracy. In tsarist Russia such aims, too, were revolutionary. These various revolutionary groups were joined by representatives of Russia's numerous national minorities, who demanded equality, autonomy, self-determination, and similar rights which tsarist Russia denied them. These classes were revolutionary in the sense that their grievances were deep and the system was unable or too dilatory to satisfy them. My calling them "revolutionary" does not, however, mean that Russia's peasants, workers, and growing middle class were active in fomenting revolution or even desirous of overthrowing tsarism. On the contrary, the vast majority of Russians doubtless felt that their needs and hopes could and would be satisfied by the tsar and his government. Only dramatic crises of confidence jolted sufficient numbers out of this belief to cause revolutionary upheavals.

Russia had witnessed rebellion, unrest, and revolution throughout the ages. But the revolutions of 1905 and 1917 were unique because in them for the first time the entire people, or at least the vast majority, participated actively or tolerated the upheaval passively. These revolutions were different also because, unlike most previous rebellions Russia had witnessed, they were fought in the name of ideals imported from the West: the ideals of liberalism and socialism. Finally, in 1917, these ideals were being propounded and translated into programs and strategies by organized political parties well known to the broad masses of the population.

Nineteenth-century Russia had proved to be curiously receptive to the most radical Western ideas; and, beginning in the 1880's, Marxism began to exert tremendous influence on the minds of revolutionary intellectuals. Out of local conspiratorial organizations, which often began to coalesce with the spontaneously growing labor movement, a Marxist party was born which by 1903 emerged fully organized, though troubled by serious disagreements. In fact, we can easily agree with Leopold Haimson, who says that the Russian Social-Democratic Labor Party in 1903 was stillborn: the disagreements dividing the party in the very beginning of its history became more and more acute. Factions developed into separate parties; and the contending leaders finally found themselves on opposite sides of the barricades.

These disagreements can be traced to the difficulties that inevitably arose when attempts were made to apply Marxist ideas to Russia. It should be obvious that the thoughts of Marx and Engels about the nature of the revolution or about political strategy could not serve as an adequate guide to their Russian disciples. Marxism was the product of Western conditions and Western developments; and many features of Russian society did not correspond to the Marxist model. Marx and Engels had relied on a large and mature proletariat to seize power when the number of capitalists had been reduced to a minimum. In Russia, however, the number of workers was small in comparison with the total population. Moreover, capitalism, far from being on the decline or even at its peak, was still growing. The number of people engaged in business was small; not, however, because competition had ruined most of them, but, rather, because Russian capitalism was still in its beginnings. Russia remained overwhelmingly a country of peasants. Who was to serve as the historical moving force in such a country? Who was to play the revolutionary role most Marxists wanted to be played?

And what kind of revolution was it to be? It could not very well be expected that a proletarian revolution in Russia—or any revolution whatsoever—would usher in the socialist society predicted by Marx and Engels. Russia's peasant society could not produce that abundance of industrial products which, in Marxist theory, is one of the essential preconditions of socialism. Hence even a proletarian revolution in Russia would have to have different results from those expected in the West.

Every one of these and related questions raised controversies that created and exacerbated division in the Russian Marxist movement. Obviously, it would not be possible within the framework of this study to trace any of these controversies. Since our topic is communism, we must, in any event, largely disregard the arguments of noncommunist Marxists. Hence we will not be able to discuss the views of the mensheviks at all. But even the bolsheviks' views can be summarized only in the sketchiest manner.[2]

Bolsheviks and mensheviks agreed that in Russia the working class must fight for not one but two revolutions —the bourgeois and the proletarian one. Their political program thus gave unprecedentedly sharp emphasis to the Marxist distinction between maximal and minimal goals. The bolsheviks' minimum program aimed to destroy tsarism and the rule of landlords, and to establish a "democratic republic," that is, a constitutional, representative government, in which, to be sure, social legislation providing for social security, minimum wages, maximum hours, and the like, was to protect the working class against excessive exploitation. Only after this stage had been reached would it be advisable to begin preparations for the proletarian revolution that would usher in the socialist society.

This step-by-step approach to socialism was dictated by the developmental theory of Marxism, which sees history as a logical unfolding of stages, where the contradictions or inconsistencies inherent in each stage determine the nature of the succeeding one. Few Marxists even in Russia were prepared to admit the possibility that any major stage might be skipped altogether, though in practice communist theory was to come close to this position, as we shall see.

The communists' endeavor to help establish a "democratic republic" in Russia can be explained by another argument as well: Communism was convinced (and com-

munists today tend to have similar convictions) that constitutional democracy was more desirable than the tsarist
police state or any other autocratic government.

The communist attitude toward democracy is highly
complex. In the sense of popular government, democracy
is, of course, part of the ideal toward which Marxism and
Leninism are striving. The idea of the withering away of
government in favor of some sort of anarchic communal-
ism is but the most radical formulation of democratic
ideals, as Marx himself was eager to point out. It was
to be accomplished by abolishing the rule of special interests (ruling classes), which alone, in the eyes of Marx,
made the existence of repressive governmental institutions necessary. Once classes were abolished, repressive
institutions would become unnecessary and would gradually disappear. In Marxist theory, the fulfillment of the
liberal ideal is thus seen as a by-product of the fulfillment
of socialist ideals. All these notions live on in present-day
communist thought. As a matter of fact, the concept of
the withering away of the state is receiving renewed attention in Soviet theoretical literature, since the Kremlin
has announced that the transition from socialism to communism is now in process.[3]

But there has been controversy within the communist
camp over the question whether the classless society, and
the democracy that goes with it, can be attained through
democratic processes of representative, constitutional government. On the one hand, Marxism is based on the belief that the working class is rational. A consequence of
this belief is a general faith in democratic processes; and
for this reason Marxist politicians have generally been
in favor of constitutional government, widening of the
franchise, civil liberties, and the like. These rights and advantages might have to be won by a revolution (which
would, of course, be the bourgeois revolution). But, once
won, they would assure the victory of the proletariat. Or,
rather, once constitutional democracy was fully realized,
the proletariat, constituting the vast majority of the people, would be in power. Engels could therefore say that

the democratic republic would be the specific form of the dictatorship of the proletariat.

The Russian communists could not follow Marx and Engels all the way in these thoughts. For in Russia, where the proletariat was still in the minority, the democratic republic would not spell proletarian rule. Yet, untrammeled democracy could nonetheless be very useful to the proletarian movement as a stepping stone toward the proletarian dictatorship, and for this reason it was the main plank of the minimum platform. We can best understand this if we realize that Russian revolutionary intellectuals instinctively contrasted the word "democracy" with autocracy and bureaucracy. To them, it therefore signified not so much constitutional government or any government whatsoever, but rather the absence of restraint. Like Marx, they interpreted the concept of democracy in the spirit of Rousseau rather than Madison. According to Marxist theory, however, the absence of governmental restraints in capitalist society could mean only open class warfare; for the absence of such restraints would cause all the contradictions of capitalism to come to the surface and clearly divide society. Democracy therefore becomes synonymous with civil war. Such a clear and open struggle, however, would be desirable because it could end only with the victory of the proletariat.

To be sure, communist strategy also took into account the fact that democratic government can be equated with constitutional, representative government, which customarily provides political liberties for all citizens; and the establishment of such a government in place of more authoritarian forms is desirable because the communist movement, like all interest groups, would like to operate as freely as possible.* Moreover, the struggle for political liberties would benefit the communist movement whether it was successful or not. Success would give desired advan-

---

* The fact that the communist movement would like to enjoy the benefits of constitutionalism only in order to supplant the constitutional order by a proletarian dictatorship is irrelevant in this context.

tages. Failure could be used for the purpose of buttressing the communists' argument that under capitalism democracy will always be imperfect.

Hence communism fights with unrelenting vigor to establish and perfect constitutional democracy. Win or lose, the fight will pay off. And yet, we can detect a certain hesitancy about this, a certain preference for losing the fight. For communism has remained highly suspicious of the liberties granted under constitutional government. While democratic institutions might be regarded as an aid in revolutionary struggle, communists warn that a Marxist should never fall victim to "constitutional illusions," that is, to the belief that capitalism can be overthrown and socialism established without violence and revolution. Bourgeois democracy, wrote Lenin, "is always narrow, hypocritical, mendacious, and false; it always remains democracy for the rich, a bluff for the poor." [4] While he criticized those of his comrades who did not recognize the advantages of utilizing the freedoms of representative government, he was even more critical of those who thought that the fight for democratic liberties was an end in itself. Such an overemphasis of the minimum program, he thought, amounted to a betrayal of the proletarian revolution. Communism thus has a highly ambivalent attitude toward piecemeal gains: they are useful and must be used; but they also threaten to corrupt those who gain advantages from them.

The precise relationship of their minimum goal to the final and over-all aims of the movement was not the only problem troubling the Russian communists. Circumstances also caused them at various times to redefine the minimum goal itself: although in their purist moods communist theoreticians have asserted that there is no essential difference between various types of capitalist society, practical politics impelled them at other times to voice a preference for one or another such type as the minimal goal to strive for. Furthermore, it has always been a thorny problem for them to decide precisely what forces in underdeveloped societies such as Russia were to carry out this bourgeous revolution. Russian communists were agreed that in their country the *bourgeois revolution* would have to be carried out or at least initiated and led *by the proletariat*—a curious but extremely important variation on the original Marxist theme. But, obviously, a proletariat constituting a small minority could not by itself carry out this revolution. Who should be its allies? And how should such allies be attracted to the party of the proletariat? In answering these questions communism has played it by ear; but, after a good deal of controversy, the Russian pattern of 1917 has emerged as the school solution: according to this pattern, the proletariat is to carry out the bourgeois revolution aided by the land-hungry peasantry, by dissatisfied national or other minorities, and possibly even by sections of the liberal middle class wherever this class can be expected to be ready for revolutionary action. The proletariat is to attract these auxiliary forces by adopting their specific grievances and aspirations as planks in its own political platform and is to promote these aspirations in the most vigorous and radical fashion, so as to steal all other revolutionary parties' thunder. Communist programs in underdeveloped countries therefore typically include demands for radical land reform and for national self-determination.

While stressing the need for alliances and for the theoretical and political flexibility that would make such alliances possible, communist doctrine stresses even more the idea that in all such political arrangements the proletariat must retain a leading role. Proletarian hegemony in the bourgeois revolution, paradoxical as it may sound, is demanded by communist strategy for several reasons. For one thing, Lenin was convinced that, in Russia at least, the bourgeoisie was not interested enough in "its own" revolution to promote it without being pushed by the working class; or, as a variant of this, he tended to believe that precisely because of vigorous proletarian initiative the bourgeoisie was not interested. In any event, he assumed that the bourgeoisie could not be expected to promote the bourgeois revolution. And, once the revolution had begun, the bourgeoisie could be expected to work against it or to betray it by making compromises with the old ruling class. Finally, he argued that proletarian hegemony in the bourgeois revolution would ease the transition to the next stage—the proletarian revolution.

We are touching here yet another problem concerning the relationship between the two revolutions: How can the party make sure that the transition from the bourgeois to a socialist society is effected most swiftly and efficiently? For, after all, as soon as it has been reached, the minimum goal turns into an obstacle, into something hostile that must be overcome; or, at best, it is regarded as a stepping stone toward the higher goal. In no case, however, is it something desirable in its own right. On the contrary, the longer the phase between the bourgeois revolution and the proletarian revolution lasts, the more time given the bourgeois regime to entrench itself, the more difficult will it be to complete the series of revolutions. Communist theory has remained ambiguous about this problem. Estimates of the desirable or probable time span that would separate one from the other have ranged from Vladimir Lenin's "era of world wars and revolutions" to Leon Trotsky's hope that the two revolutions might merge and occur simultaneously, an idea which was based on thoughts vaguely expressed by Marx and Engels in the *Communist Manifesto*. (Even the Trotskyist term "permanent revolution" was used by Marx and Engels in this context.) In between we have another idea of Lenin's, namely, that the democratic republic established by the proletariat in the bourgeois revolution would slowly but surely "grow over" into socialism.

The Marxist-Leninist program for Russia was further refined and complicated by linking it with the expected world revolution—partly in order better to justify revolutionary action by the Marxist movement in a backward country. Many of the daring schemes constituting the Russian communist program were so bold a departure from the original Marxist scheme that many other Marxist theoreticians looked upon Lenin's party as a group of unprincipled adventurers lusting for power regardless of the consequences. They argued that Russia was in no wise prepared (or "mature") for a proletarian regime, and that therefore a Russian revolution carried out under proletarian hegemony could not but lead to failure and would discredit the entire Marxist movement.

Communists agreed that a proletarian revolution in Russia made no sense. Yet when the chance came to seize power, they seized it in the name of the proletariat. But, whether or not they were in fact unprincipled adventurers, they did have a theoretical justification for their action. I have called the arguments they used the theory of the spark. Just as Lenin insisted that the working class as the most conscious element of society would set the bourgeois revolution in motion by its own initiative, so he asserted that the proletarian revolution in Russia (doomed to failure if it were an isolated event) would spark a world-wide chain reaction of proletarian revolution. This world revolution, in turn, would ensure the success of socialism even in such a backward country as Russia. Here we see that even in Lenin's view the bourgeois and the proletarian revolutions have merged into one event.

The Party

Marx and Engels were concerned primarily with prognoses, that is, trends of development they thought they recognized in present-day reality. Lenin, however, stressed plans and wishes, goals and desiderata. Marx and Engels were confident that reality would develop toward the goal. Lenin knew what the goal was and made the most determined efforts to reach it. To be sure, they all asserted the inevitability of socialism. But I think that we can detect a subtle change in this notion of inevitability. For Marx and Engels it had been a concrete certainty of events to come in the immediate future. For Lenin it was far more theoretical than that. And theory in this case was always in danger of being divorced from practice. Theoretically socialism was inevitable; any convinced

Marxist was sure of that. But practically it would take careful planning and adjustments to make it come about. Theory, in short, was no longer an expression of what was, that is, scientific analysis and description; instead, it had become a guide to action, a method of analyzing and understanding reality in such a fashion that it could be used for the attainment of the goals the theory had developed.

By emphasizing goals, communism prepared to discard the means, procedures, and patterns of development that Marx and Engels had foreseen or described. The validity of their scheme of evolution was never challenged directly, but in the hands of communist political leaders it became more and more schematic and abstract. At the same time, communist theory gave even greater emphasis than Marx and Engels had given to theory itself as a creative force in history, or, as Lenin would have said, to *consciousness*.

Communism is a school of Marxism which assigns a tremendously important role to rational understanding, which they call consciousness. To communists it is the most essential force in history. For, without scientific knowledge, or, rather, without leadership by people possessing such knowledge, chaos and disaster instead of socialism might be the outcome of history.

Communism complements its demand for proletarian hegemony with the equally insistent striving for the hegemony of consciousness. Hegemony over what? Over insufficiently developed consciousness, that is, over instinct, habit, tradition—in short over any political action which is not based on the scientific (read: Marxist) understanding of reality. Communist theory defines nonconscious political action as *spontaneous;* and the hegemony of consciousness is therefore to be established over spontaneity.

Conceptually, this is not different from the Marxist theory, in which the proletariat was assigned its Chosen People role precisely because consciousness was attributed to it. Because Marx did attribute consciousness to the working class, however, he had no need to differentiate theoretically between consciousness and spontaneity. The *Communist Manifesto* refers to the party as an organization providing theoretical and practical leadership and mentions bourgeois intellectuals who, by virtue of their enlightenment and insight, break away from their own class and provide this leadership for the proletariat. But the implication remains nonetheless that the spontaneous emergence of class consciousness in the proletariat itself is inevitable. Consciousness and spontaneity coincide in the theory of Marx and Engels.

In Leninist theory they do not. On the contrary, by itself (that means spontaneously) the working class would never attain consciousness. Consequently, it would never be able to carry out its historic task.

Nonetheless, consciousness must guide the proletariat. And if the working class by itself cannot attain it, it must be found elsewhere. Lenin asserted that it was possessed by educated people, intellectuals such as he. It is they whom consciousness compels to prepare and lead the proletariat in the revolutions that have to be staged in Russia. They are expected to provide this leadership by devoting their entire lives to the task, becoming revolutionaries by profession. They are the ones who should form the party, which Lenin conceived as consciousness incarnate or institutionalized, the *Ecclesia Militans* of history, the general staff of the proletarian revolutions. And, because Leninism relies so firmly on consciousness for deliverance, it must rely with equal fervor on the strength and the survival of the party in which consciousness has become flesh. Come what may, the party must be preserved. Without it the proletariat is nothing. Without it everything is lost.

A general staff by itself, however, cannot wage nor win a battle. A party formed only by the enlightened few is unable to win revolutions. To do so, the vanguard of the proletariat must be sure that the rank and file of the working class will act according to its commands. In addition, the party must aim to go beyond the working class in at-

tracting the allies which, as we have seen, the proletariat
in backward countries need.

All political parties seek to gain adherents and become
decisive majorities. In order to do so, parties customarily
try to develop programs and voice slogans that respond to
the felt or anticipated needs of potential political adherents. They try to voice the will of the people or of important groups within the people.

The Communist Party cannot gain adherents quite so
simply. Since it believes that it is the repository of consciousness, while the people, including even the proletariat, are incapable of defining their own interests, the party
obviously cannot let the "spontaneous" feelings of the
masses determine policy. On the contrary, its consciousness, and the goals and policies derived from it, must
somehow be instilled in, or imposed on, the people whom
the party wishes to lead. What is required, then, is an educational job; and indeed the party regards its most important function to be the education of the proletariat. The
consciousness which the party possesses must be given
to the working class.

Communist theorists refer to this educational work as
"propaganda," but they do not wish to imply by the use
of this word irrational, tricky, or deceptive means of persuasion. On the contrary, propaganda denotes the painful
and lengthy effort of so educating the proletariat that it
understands and absorbs Marxist theory in all its ramifications and complications. For only this constitutes consciousness. There are, however, means short of this difficult process, which the party uses to gain adherents.
There are, for instance, the important first steps of the
educational effort, measures designed to wake up the
masses and plant the first seeds of consciousness in their
minds. These first steps are short and simple messages—
slogans—dramatizing the workers' grievances and providing greatly simplified explanations for them. Collectively,
these primitive efforts to arouse resentment against capitalism and faith in communism are called "agitation." Its
messages are no more meant to be deceptive than those

of propaganda; they are only simplified truths which even simple minds can grasp.

Yet, education to consciousness is not enough. Communist theorists have great difficulty deciding how much effort and time is required to raise the workers' level of consciousness. Estimates have varied according to circumstances. In times of revolution or impending revolution, the party has tended to be optimistic about this problem. At other times, its leaders were aware of the difficulties they faced in educating the masses.

Yet the party needs the masses to carry out its policies. Moreover, communism is impatient Marxism, which cannot afford to wait for the proletariat to become mature, just as in Russia it could not wait until the society had finally caught up with Western Europe in its development. This impatience is the result of suppressed but strong and persistent doubts concerning the inevitability of socialism, doubts which in their turn are related not only to the unpropitious Russian environment but also to those changes in the nature of the working-class movement that led to the changes in Western Marxist doctrines (see Chapter 3). More generally yet, these doubts are a product of that era of "imperialism" which, as we will see, communist theory analyzes as the current stage of capitalist development. All these doubts have, as I phrased it above, made the idea of the inevitability of socialism more "theoretical."

Under the impact of the transformation of capitalism into imperialism and of the working class into an antirevolutionary interest group, Marxist theorists in the West abandoned revolutionary change. The Leninist solution of the same problem was different. Unwilling and, under Russian conditions, probably unable to abandon revolution as the means to attain socialism, communism found itself compelled to supplement the time-consuming method of education with more immediately effective manipulation of the masses. The party formulates goals and strategies. All that the masses have to do is to act according to the party's directives. To the communist it does not really matter whether or not the masses understand what they are doing. It may be desirable and preferable, but it is not essential.

Communism attributes consciousness to an elite of professional revolutionaries organized in the party. This party almost desperately feels the urge to act, so as to make its theory come true. Hence the masses, and in particular the proletariat, which in Marxist theory was the main agent of historic change, now turns into the main tool of such change. They become instruments in the hands of the conscious vanguard, raw material of revolutionary history, which must be molded and shaped and sent into action according to the party's plans.

The party's principal means for working with this human raw material is not, as many might suppose, propaganda (now meaning the use of irrational or deceptive means of persuasion), even though in fact there is no firm line between honest conviction and calculated appeal in the propaganda and agitation messages of communism. Moreover, many policies (apart from propaganda or education) are adopted by the party, not for their own sake, but only because they are apt to attract followers and sympathizers; or because not adopting them would disillusion those whose sympathies already are with the party. As a matter of fact, communism is often torn by a sharp dilemma: Should the party remain true to its convictions even though its orthodox stand will alienate its followers; or should it be flexible, opportunistic, obedient in some fashion to grass-roots opinion, in order to attract the masses? Unwilling to wait until the masses become conscious, the party has usually decided that some concessions to their opinions must be made. Propaganda, in the sense of manipulation, thus plays its role. But another method of manipulating the masses is far more important and desirable, because it requires no concessions to grass-roots spontaneity. That method is organization.

Lenin, in some ways rather old-fashioned, was nonetheless up-to-date in a number of ways. One trait that made him a pioneer of twentieth-century politics was his insight into the crucial role of organization. Lenin realized that in modern industrial society (if not everywhere else) man is never an isolated individual. All human activities, economic, political, recreational, educational, and so forth, are carried out in and through organizations and associations. Each individual is a functioning member of society only as a member of the various groups to which he belongs. And much of his behavior is influenced by these groups. Lenin concluded from this that masses of people could be influenced and manipulated most effectively if the manipulators were in control of the organizations and associations to which these masses belonged. Once the party controlled them, these organizations would become transmission belts (to use Lenin's phrase) conveying the will and impetus of the party leaders to the masses. Organization would be a system of wires the party could pull to set the people dancing to its tune. In this relationship, the lack of consciousness on the part of the masses did not really matter.

The Leninist party is therefore far more than a small elite of professional revolutionaries organized as leaders because they consider themselves conscious. It is also an educational institution aiming to raise the working class to the level of consciousness; and, finally, it is the center of a vast network of what we would today call front organizations, reaching, ideally, into every part of society in an attempt to control the entire associational life of broad masses of the population. The party's ideal is, of course, to dominate all of society in this indirect fashion. Needless to say, this dream comes close to being realized only after the party has come to power. Then, however, it becomes one of the guiding principles of communist government.*

Decision-making Processes

The manipulative attitude with which we have become acquainted here is at the basis of the party's ideas on or-

* See Chapter 9.

ganization, and it pervades and shapes the party's political strategy. The party views not only the working classes as political raw material that should be organized and controlled; it similarly views all forces, arrangements, institutions—in short, everything that exists in contemporary society. In principle, the communist is ready and eager to regard everything as a potential instrument which, if wielded correctly and kept under control, can serve his party's and the movement's interests. Here we see a tendency toward the dissolution of the Marxist scheme of action into Machiavellian opportunism and amoral ruthlessness. And yet, this flexibility of strategy, this readiness to adjust action to the given environment, is neither unprincipled nor un-Marxist. Whatever the communist may do, he feels guided by principles insofar as he wants to work for the proletarian revolution and for socialism. Meanwhile, whatever his strategies, the communist can remain a Marxist as long as he keeps analyzing his environment in Marxist terms. Whatever he does, Marxism remains a guide to his action as long as it guides his thinking.*

Communist theorists would strongly repudiate the inference that their movement is immoral or even amoral; on the contrary, they would stress the moral probity of communism and would claim that communist morality is the only valid morality of the contemporary world. They

---

* Other writers disagree with this, having reduced communism to purely Machiavellian principles of expediency or to a code of behavior derived from irrational attitudes closely akin to paranoia (see Nathan Leites, *A Study of Bolshevism*, Chicago, 1953). These writers see communism as pursuing only one aim—power unlimited in scope and area. In their view, communism is absolutely unprincipled and immoral, the ideology serving only as rationalization of the urge to dominate. Most popular and journalistic books on the subject take this line, which I believe is based on inadequate understanding of the nature and history of bolshevism. A recent example of such journalistic work is the much-ballyhooed book by H. and B. Overstreet, *What We Must Know About Communism* (New York, 1958). Once this view is accepted, the study of the development of communist ideas becomes, of course, quite irrelevant.

would point out that communism is based on, and in a broad sense guided by, moral indignation over capitalist inhumanity and by moral ideals concerning a society worthy of man; and communists are ever ready to measure others by their moral yardstick. The communist movement, moreover, is eager and impatient to make its ideal into reality. It wants action and success. Success in an evil world, however, is attainable only by working within that world and using the means that are at the movement's disposal. The *practical* morality of the communist movement is therefore a morality of expediency: whatever works is moral; whatever does not, is immoral. Whoever because of moral scruples fails to act resolutely to bring socialism nearer is a traitor to the morally just cause of communism. Whoever overcomes his "petty-bourgeois" moral scruples, whoever is unafraid to dirty his hands in the noble work of removing obstacles in the path of moral progress, is worthy of praise. Communism thus adopts the old maxim first attributed to the Jesuits, that the end justifies the means. It need hardly be pointed out that this contradicts prevalent Western notions of morality.[5]

At the same time, the manipulative attitude makes it more and more difficult to make decisions and to determine precisely what the proper Marxist course would be. The reason for this is that the manipulative attitude is linked with a profound ambivalence toward everything that exists. Everything—classes, groups, nations, institutions, attitudes, traditions—everything is potentially useful to the party. But everything is at the same time part of the hated present. Everything is both an obstacle and a stepping stone on the road to progress. And Marxist theory, being highly abstract, cannot really guide the party leader in deciding how positively or negatively he is to judge any phenomenon at any particular time. After all, Marx and Engels themselves did not always agree on such appraisals.

This ambivalence is intensified by the fact that the communist thinks on several levels of abstraction at one and the same time. Not only that, he must plan his course

of action on several different levels—maximum and minimum programs; strategy and tactics; action based on
principles as against that which is an accommodation to
special circumstances; action in different locales. Obviously, various courses of action are open to the party in
any one situation, all of them fully consonant with
Marxist-Leninist theory.

To prevent paralysis or chaos, therefore, more than
theoretical skills (consciousness) is required. According
to Lenin's principles, consciousness must be linked to an
efficient decision-making machinery—a party government
—so as to make sure that in every case the correct decision is made. And that for every situation there is one and
only one correct decision Lenin was convinced, even
though it seems, in the light of what we have discussed
above, this conviction cannot be reconciled with the ambivalent (dialectical) and multilevel approach to reality
characterizing Marxism. To be sure, Marx and Engels
themselves, however prone they were on the basis of their
method to regard the world in contradictory terms, were
often as dogmatic as Lenin when discussing courses of
action. In their cases, too, we get the impression that they
recognized only one solution to a problem as correct.

Lenin, moreover, was a rare type of revolutionary: a
revolutionary with a bureaucratic mind. Such a combination is rare because most revolutionaries so hate the bureaucracy of the social system they want to overthrow
that they come to hate all officialdom. Certainly, in the
political thought of Western liberalism, which is suspicious of all governmental authority, this is true; and
Marxism, being an heir to the liberal heritage, shares its
antibureaucratic bias in the main. Lenin, however, as a
rule did not share it. He seems to have felt that there was
something inherently rational in good bureaucratic organization; that such organization, when put to work, would
produce correct decisions, especially when it consisted
of conscious people. It may very well be that this faith
in rational organization only covered up his desire to create a governmental apparatus completely subservient to

him; perhaps he was organization-happy because it suited his purposes. I for one believe that this is part of the truth. But another part is the fact that Lenin's preoccupation with principles and problems of centralized bureaucratic organization is in tune with the beliefs and preconceptions of Marx and Engels. After all, as prophets of the cult of rationality and the good life in this world, they praised not only the machine age, but also collectivism and large-scale, centralized administration. In their eyes, these were aspects of up-to-date civilization, which in the socialist society would be preserved and fostered.* Still, Lenin's motivation is rather irrelevant. What counts, for the history and development of communism, are the principles of organization which emerged.

Lenin wanted the party to be a striking organization which could be totally committed to any action as quickly as possible. He wanted this organization to be absolutely centralized and subject to firm control by its leaders. He wanted its organization to be hierarchical, following the command principle of armed forces, where the chief virtue of the lower ranks is discipline and obedience. Comparison of the party with a military organization is not a far-fetched idea attributable to Western critics. On the contrary, Lenin made it clear that military organization was the pattern according to which he wished the party to be organized. Communist ideologists have a predilection for military terminology. The revolutions they promote are battles to be fought and won; the societies within which they occur are fronts in a global war; the workers are the rank-and-file soldiers; other classes furnish reserve troops; and the party is the general staff.

But the conception of the party as a disciplined bureaucratic body was in sharp conflict with another principle of organization: the democratic one. That the proletarian movement should organize itself and manage its own af-

* If I have drawn a contradictory picture of Marxist attitudes toward bureaucracy, I have done so in the awareness that one must not expect political philosophies to be altogether consistent.

fairs democratically follows logically from the assumption
that the proletariat is conscious. And if that assumption
is replaced by one which attributes consciousness only to
the party elite, then democracy should reign within that
vanguard of the elect. For, surely, where everyone is conscious, everyone's voice should be heard; and everyone's
counsel is of equal worth. Not even Lenin ever saw fit to
repudiate this argument.

Bureaucratic-authoritarian principles of organization
thus were in conflict with democratic ones. Lenin attempted to resolve this clash by a formula: the party, he
argued, should be governed in accordance with the principle of "democratic centralism."

The formula symbolizes the desire to merge both principles. According to Lenin, party policies should be formulated by absolutely free discussion and deliberation,
with every party member entitled to participate either directly or through freely elected representatives. The formal structure of the party corresponds to this, in that the
sovereign body which, in theory, determines policy is the
party Congress of delegates representing the entire membership. All executive organizations of the party, such as
the Central Committee and its numerous subsidiary or
servant organizations are, formally, accountable to the
Congress. In addition to providing for free discussion of
all pending questions, the democratic element of democratic centralism was meant to give each individual party
member freedom to criticize. Indeed, Lenin once defined
democratic centralism as "freedom to criticize and unity
in action." The centralistic principle of "unity in action"
was to prevail only after policies had been adopted and
had become party law. Then, after every member had had
his opportunity to speak up, all dissent was to be suppressed and the party was to display monolithic unity.
Any sign of disagreement at such a time was to be regarded as an unpardonable breach of discipline and punished by expulsion. A party committed in action could not
tolerate dissenters within its ranks.

Thus freedom to criticize was obviously to be sharply

circumscribed. But exactly how to circumscribe it remained a problem. To be legitimate, said the party leaders, criticism should be constructive. But what is the criterion of constructiveness? Criticism, said the party rules, should focus on the execution of adopted policies rather than on the policies themselves. *What* was being done should be beyond criticism; only *how* it was being done could be a matter of dispute. But the borderline between policy formulation and policy execution does not exist except in textbooks. In practice it is meaningless. Moreover, who is to have the right to challenge policies that have been in force for a long time, or for any length of time? Somebody must be able to point out that circumstances have changed and that measures once adopted unanimously have outlived their usefulness. Someone must be authorized to prepare agendas for meetings and congresses and thereby indicate what problems deserve to be discussed. But, according to the rules of centralism and discipline, such suggestions ought not to be made by any member while the party is committed in action. Yet, is not the party always committed? Is there ever a moment when dissent is not dangerous and a breach of discipline and unanimity?

The cards were stacked overwhelmingly against democratic principles. Lenin may have paid lip service to them; he may even have been completely sincere in his praises of party democracy. But he was also highly impatient with criticism and dissent. He was contemptuous or perhaps even fearful of Russian intellectuals and their proverbial knack for interminable and aimless discussion. He wanted action rather than words, results instead of dreams. And to attain these aims he favored centralism and authoritarianism.

In addition to Lenin's tremendous prestige within the party, two devices became important in curbing democracy. One was a rule outlawing "factionalism," adopted at the Tenth Party Congress in 1921, which had the effect of atomizing all dissent. Disagreement and criticism could still be voiced; but it had to be voiced by indi-

viduals. The formation of dissenting groups, the writing of
minority reports or rival platforms, even the organization
of minority discussion groups were outlawed as treason
against the party. These formal curbs on the freedom of
discussion were supplemented by an increasing tendency
on the part of the leaders to control the membership
through the party's administrative organs, to make the
representative gatherings more and more subservient to
the party bureaucracy, to pack them with yes men, and
the like. Centralism consequently won a complete victory
over party democracy.

World View

The composite picture of the Leninist or communist, as
an ideal type, reveals a radical, revolutionary Marxist, imbued with loathing for capitalism and yearning for socialism, and in a hurry to attain this goal; ruthless in his methods and opportunistic in his strategies; absolutely loyal to
his party and its leaders, and filled with holy intolerance
of any ideas or even facts that might shake his loyalty;
ever eager to deepen his own consciousness, yet disciplined and obedient as a party servant. When Lenin or his
followers talked about "hard" Marxists or "hard" bolsheviks, they had in mind that combination of ruthlessness
and devotion, of unscrupulousness and unquestioning loyalty. As we shall see when we discuss the history of the
party, they did not always get the kind of following they
wanted, and the party at various times also attracted people who had only one or two of the desired traits. The
ideal bolshevik, however, is as hard as he is radical, and
the combination of these traits is a syndrome that distinguishes him from most other parties of either the right
or the left. To make the image more complete, however,
we shall have to describe his general world view. By that
I mean not his philosophy but his image of society in the
twentieth century.

For the communist, ours is the age of *imperialism;* and
in order to understand what this implies, we have to

determine what the term "imperialism" means in communist writings. For this purpose, we shall have to begin by sketching the circumstances under which the term gained currency.

The word began to be used around the beginning of our century, when the expansion of the European powers into economically backward and politically defenseless areas of Asia and Africa had reached its peak. New colonial empires were established at that time; spheres of influence and domination were carved out; and fierce rivalries developed between the European powers in their competition for areas of domination.

For the Western world in general, this was a period of rapid economic growth through the work of ever-larger industrial and financial corporate structures, of quickly rising living standards, and increasing national consciousness. For the Marxist movement, it was a time of puzzlement and soul searching, because so many features of their contemporary world corresponded less and less with the Marxist model as they understood it. The decline of capitalism seemed remoter than ever. The revolutionary spirit of the working class was yielding to the tendency to strive for reforms within the existing system. The entire timetable of Marxism seemed hopelessly upset. Where the spirit of revolution was still alive, it was in relatively backward countries, in which proletarian revolutions did not make much sense according to a strict and dogmatic reading of Marxism. All these developments required explanation; and the communist theory of imperialism was an attempt to provide it.[6]

Reduced to the simplest terms, this explanation runs as follows: Instead of having developed its internal contradictions and tensions to a point where a revolutionary break must occur, capitalism has found a way out of these contradictions, even though previously they were thought to be insoluble. The way out is expansion throughout the world in search of cheap raw materials, ready markets for commodities and for excess capital, and, most important, cheap labor which can be exploited in unprecedented measure. This expansion of capitalism is called imperialism.

In his attempt to describe the social processes going on in his time, Lenin further defined imperialism. He described it as an intensification of all those features that Marx and Engels had attributed to capitalism. In his law of the concentration of capital, Marx had described how the small entrepreneur is inevitably wiped out by his larger competitors and capital is concentrated in fewer and fewer hands. According to communist theory, this concentration has proceeded apace and has led to the development of *monopoly capitalism*. Similarly, the fate Marx and Engels predicted for the majority of the middle classes, namely, transformation into proletarians, has, according to Lenin, become reality; almost everyone outside a small power elite is a helpless cog in a vast commercialized machine dominated by monopolists.

But if indeed the tendencies seen by the writers of the *Communist Manifesto* have reached their peak, what is to explain the failure of the revolutionary movement and the staying power of capitalism? The communists' reply is that this intensification of various essential features of capitalism has temporarily eased some of the strains under which the system labored. First of all, the reign of monopoly and the increasing interference of centralized government in the economy reduce the anarchy which, according to Marx and Engels, characterized free-enterprise economy. Monopoly capitalism and state capitalism, as the communists call the modern Western systems, are guided and planned. Further, they argue, monopoly has grown so strong in its grip on the system that it can afford to make political concessions to the lower classes and thus tie them more firmly to the status quo. Moreover, monopoly capitalism, by exploiting backward areas, reaps such enormous profits—communist theory calls them superprofits—that it can bribe the proletariat (or at least its leaders) also with economic concessions, that is, with a rising standard of living. One of the fundamental laws of capitalist development in Marxist theory, the law of the increasing misery of the masses, is thus substantially modified. Finally, the workers have been corrupted also by the fierce nationalism which, as a result of imperialist competition, has been fostered within each imperialist nation. This nationalism, to which according to Lenin the working-class leadership especially has fallen victim, has corroded international proletarian solidarity and made the workers' movement a pawn in the hands of the ruling classes.

The chances for a proletarian revolution therefore seem more remote than ever. But Communist theory resurrects the optimism of Marx and Engels by uncovering new tendencies toward the eventual breakdown of capitalism and new revolutionary forces to speed up the process and carry it forward to construct a socialist commonwealth. This new theory of doom and renascence forms the core of the theory of imperialism.

According to communist thought, the "contradictions" of capitalism have been overcome within the Western nations only to reappear on a global scale. Within any one nation, the anarchy of capitalist production may have been reduced to a minimum. But sharp and deadly competition lives on between international monopolies and between the various imperialist nations; and on a global level capitalism is therefore as anarchic as ever. Analyzing this competition in some detail, Lenin came to the conclusion that it could be resolved only by war; and the inevitability of imperialist wars, that is, wars between various capitalist nations, remained an axiom of communist theory until very recently, even though the course of world history since 1917 had given rise to the nagging fear that a counter tendency might exist: ever since the birth of a communist regime in Russia, communist leaders have ever been in fear of a world-wide alliance of all imperialist nations in a crusade to wipe out Soviet Russia. This fear of an all-imperialist bloc and of "capitalist encirclement" has played an important role in communist ideology.

Further contradictions of capitalism are seen in imperi-

alism. For instance, capitalism, according to communist
theory, has saved itself from collapse by exporting capital
into underdeveloped areas. But, as industrial civilization
engulfs the entire globe, it becomes more and more difficult to dispose of the faster and faster accumulating
surpluses. Soon there will be no new frontiers nor safety
valves. Moreover, by exporting capital, the West also ex-
ports capital*ism* with all its stresses and its inherent revolutionary potential to areas hitherto untouched by Western
history. Not only competition but also those other features Marx had seen in capitalism—exploitation and
domination of man by man and a resulting struggle of
classes—reappear on a global scale. The new class struggle which develops in the age of imperialism, according to
communist theory, is more complicated than the conflict
between capitalists and proletarians was in the nineteenth
century. The old struggle persists, although it is mitigated
temporarily in the imperialist countries. And it now goes
on everywhere, even if only under the surface. In addition, however, world society is now divided into the exploiters and the exploited in yet another fashion: the new
exploited populations are entire nations, namely, those
backward, underdeveloped peoples on whom the capitalist world has been encroaching. Modern communist theory attributes to them the same relationship to the exploiter nations as the proletariat was to have to the
bourgeoisie. The class struggle is thus partly transformed
into an international conflict.

This picture, which has been drawn in very simplified
strokes, has interesting implications for the over-all
theory of revolution of Marx and Engels. One concept
that was very important to their earlier followers was that
of *maturity:* conditions had to be ripe for a proletarian
revolution before working-class action made sense; capitalism had to be highly developed as a social system, and
industrial technology had to be sufficiently advanced to
provide a decent livelihood for all. Then conditions would
be mature for the proletarian revolution. Now this concept is virtually turned upside down. Industrial capitalism

and the revolutionary movement are seen not as developing in direct but in inverse proportion to each other.
Highly developed industrial countries get stuck in the rut
of imperialism, while the revolution develops in backward
countries. *Consciousness is more important than the maturity of conditions*. This is one of the implications of the
communist theory of imperialism.

Another implication is the theory of "combined development." The sharp line drawn above between exploiter
nations and exploited nations does not imply that either
type is homogeneous. To be sure, in the imperialist world
the class struggle may be stifled; but it is taken for granted
by most (not all) communists that eventually it will erupt
with renewed vigor. Meanwhile in the underdeveloped
nations a far more complicated class conflict rages. For
in these societies the fight of the proletariat against the
bourgeoisie goes on simultaneously with the struggle of
peasants against landlords, bourgeois against traditional
rulers, caste against caste, nationality against nationality.
Thus backward societies, in the communist view, combine
features which in the West characterized different stages
of development. Noncontemporaneous elements here are
telescoped so as to coincide in time, because modern
civilization, through Western imperialism, has been super-
imposed on societies hitherto untouched by Western developments.

To the revolutionary strategist this phenomenon opens
up exciting new perspectives for action. It makes possible
unique combinations of social forces; it creates political
constellations of new and ever-shifting character, which
have to be examined anew in each country. And this necessity to regard every underdeveloped country as unique
in its social problems gives theoretical justification to all
the pragmatism and seeming opportunism of communist
parties. The strategies and tactics used by Marx and Engels, which used to be copied slavishly by their earlier followers, have ceased to be obligatory.

Not only do strategies and tactics become more flexible
on the basis of such theories, however; the whole concep-

tion of the revolution changes profoundly. First of all, in the communist view, the revolution is no longer to be carried out by the proletariat alone but by an alliance of the Western proletariat with the underdeveloped nations and the colonies and dependencies. Its point of departure, its origin, is no longer the condition of the working class but the condition of all mankind, seen as victims of imperialism. The crucial point of Marxism, that conditions have to be ripe for revolution, has been amended, as we have seen. The maturity of capitalism now is seen to lead to revolution, not in the capitalist world, but somewhere else. The aims of the revolution also have changed. In the *Communist Manifesto*, the proletariat was to seize the means of industrial production in the name of society and utilize them in collectivist fashion for the benefit of all. The aim of the new revolution must be different; for in underdeveloped areas there is little that can be seized, and current means of production will not suffice to satisfy the material needs of those societies. The revolution of the colonial world has as its immediate aim the destruction of imperialism. It is to weaken the rule of capital not only in the colonies but also in the home countries by knocking the props from underneath the tottering system. Having accomplished this negative task, the coming world revolution is to proceed toward an even more difficult undertaking, which is to *build* modern industrial civilization in the underdeveloped areas, to copy the achievements of the capitalist West, in order to emancipate all mankind from it. For this, strong communist governments are required; hence it would be foolish to expect that the revolution will lead at once to the withering away of oppressive institutions. On the contrary, the emerging communist states will have to emphasize dictatorship, sacrifice, and continued alienation, for entire nations will have to be reëducated to be made fit for the machine age. In this fashion, the revolution, which in the minds of Marx and Engels was to have been a comparatively brief interlude, albeit violent and bloody, now assumes much greater dimensions in time by becoming an entire era of what communists call "socialist construction." We shall have to deal with the theory and practice of communist government in the following chapters, but we shall lead up to them by first presenting a brief history of the Russian communist party from its very beginnings.

5

History of the Russian Communist Party up to the Death of Lenin

A knowledge of doctrine and the environment in which it was worked out is insufficient to give us an adequate understanding of communism. Knowledge of the history of the party as a political organization, and of the major personalities that helped make this history, is essential to understanding, for major events and milestones in the history of the party have had a lasting impact on it. This is partly because communism itself is very history conscious and tends to see present-day problems in terms of historical parallels and precedents. There is perhaps no other way of life in which historical memory (true as well as distorted) has played so important a role as a means of educating the younger generation. Or are there other creeds which use a history textbook as their main political primer and catechism? One other history textbook which has played a similar role is the Old Testament.

Russian intellectuals, disaffected and critical, were ever eager to slake their thirst for ideas about history and society and to show their disapproval of Russian conditions by adopting the most radical ideas they found in the West. The curious consequence was that the first foreign language into which Marx's major work was translated was Russian. Marxism quickly became well known among radical intellectuals and gained adherents. Young men and women met in conspiratorial groups to study and discuss Marxist literature and tried to establish contact with the working class. From the very beginning, some of the most important leaders of the new movement found themselves spending most of their lives in Western Europe, out of reach of the tsarist police and in touch with the Marxist parties of the West. With the exception of a brief period around 1905, the center of the Russian Marxist movement from its beginnings to the revolution of 1917 was to be found in Munich, Geneva, or other Western cities rather than in Moscow or St. Petersburg.

Emerging at a time when the Marxist movement in the West was entering a period of serious disputes, the Russian group was almost at once involved in struggles for the preservation of the orthodox creed. Men like Plekhanov, Akselrod, Martov, and Lenin, who belonged to the first generation of Russian Marxists, first sharpened their ideological weapons against those who maintained that Marxism was not applicable to Russia. These were primarily the Russian *narodniks*,[1] who had vague ideas about a particular native peasant socialism that could be developed in their country without Russia's having to go through a phase of capitalist development. Hardly had the Marxists succeeded in emerging from these arguments with renewed confidence in their own theory when they were forced to defend it against the Russian equivalents of the revisionists, groups opposing all political activity on the part of the working class as premature (the economists) or at least condemning all underground, subversive activity (the legal Marxists). These disputes, which in their acrimoniousness foreshadowed many subsequent arguments, were also the beginning of a never-ending process in which generation after generation of leaders were eliminated from the Russian movement.

Those who were sloughed off in these earliest battles included such pioneers of Russian Marxism as Tugan-Baranovsky and Struve.*

Among the faithful, meanwhile, important discussions set the stage for future developments and future conflicts. At stake were the formulation of a party program and the shape of the party organization; and both questions were intertwined not only with each other but also with personality conflicts and struggles for influence. Obviously questions regarding the relationship between intellectuals and workers within the party, between the party and the labor unions, between constitutional and subversive political activity, between the party headquarters and the party press, between the Russian party and the workers' movements of Russia's national minorities—all were questions that concerned both organization and party programs.

Having been founded, formally, at the otherwise rather unimportant Congress at Minsk, in 1898, the party came together in 1903 for its first major gathering in its Western-European exile. At this Second Congress the antagonism that had been developing burst into the open. The Congress turned out to be a stormy one. One group of delegates stalked out; friendships were broken; and, most important, the two major factions, mensheviks and bolsheviks, emerged, which were to divide the party perpetually. The Russian Social-Democratic Labor Party thus came out of its first important meeting split in two. There is a good deal of evidence, though perhaps none that is conclusive, that the split was deliberately provoked and

* Western scholarship in the field tends to concentrate its attention on those who have left the Marxist movement or on those who have come to oppose party authorities, and to neglect those who stayed with it or who remained as authoritative spokesmen. This is understandable, both from the point of view of human interest and from the Western political point of view. Moreover, the faithful often seem less worthy of our attention, being often the more dogmatic, less intellectual organization men. Future generations of historians will doubtless concentrate more on the successful.

engineered by Lenin, who was alarmed at the stand taken
by his antagonists within the party leadership on a whole
number of policy questions. Lenin always considered it
all-important to have a party which followed correct policies; and if the party as it existed at any given moment did
not, then it would be better to destroy it, or, rather, split
it so as to cast out those who in his opinion were mislead-
ing it. In the eyes of his antagonists, these attempts were
tantamount to wrecking the party for the sake of attaining
exclusive command over it. In their eyes, Lenin was will-
fully destroying proletarian unity and therefore wrecking
the working-class movement. Lenin's own view was, of
course, that he was only cleansing the movement of dangerous, misguided leaders who in effect were betraying
Marxism. We see that there was an irreconcilable clash
of views here. And yet, for almost another decade after
the Second Congress, the two factions nominally remained
in the same party.

The war of 1904 and, much more, the revolution of
1905 seemed at first to provide an opportunity for patch-
ing up the rift. For the masses of workers, students, and
others who during the revolution associated themselves
with the Marxist movement, the struggles and disputes
among the leaders were often meaningless; some of them
had not even heard of mensheviks and bolsheviks. Among
the rank and file of party members, there was a tendency
toward unity. This was strengthened by the fact that the
revolution temporarily eclipsed the leaders, most of whom
had difficulty getting into Russia from their places of
European exile and were able to assume command only in
the last stages of the revolution. One exception was Leon
Trotsky, who emerged in the revolution as one of the
most glamorous figures of the Russian Marxist movement.
Finally, the revolutionary upheavals themselves rendered
some of the controversies obsolete and senseless. In some
of the most important events of the revolution, such as the
armed uprising that took place in Moscow in December of
1905, bolsheviks and mensheviks collaborated without
great difficulties.

Once the revolution was defeated, however, disputes broke out with renewed vigor. Bolshevik post-mortems conflicted with menshevik ones. Even greater were the conflicts over the lessons to be drawn from the experience and over the strategies, tactics, programs, and organizational patterns to be adopted on the basis of these lessons. The so-called Unity Congress of the party, held in Stockholm in 1906, where these matters were discussed, deepened the rift. So, finally, did the bitter disputes that broke out over party finances, including not only the unorthodox manner in which the bolsheviks obtained their funds, such as bank robberies and holdups, but also the question of who should dispose of the funds.[2]

Struggles over control of finances appear to have led also to the first major rift in the leadership of the bolshevik faction, that is, between Lenin on the one hand, and Bogdanov and Krasin on the other—the triumvirate which in the years immediately after the 1905 revolution constituted the command of the bolsheviks. Conflicts over funds were complicated by philosophical disputes and by controversies over attempts either to widen or to mend the split within the entire Marxist camp. Lenin fiercely attacked those bolsheviks who sought a reconciliation and were prepared to make compromises with the mensheviks; and he resisted with equal vehemence the efforts of people standing between or above the two factions, such as Trotsky, to pave the way for a reconciliation.

The years 1910–1912 mark the breakdown of reconciliatory efforts and the emergence of the bolshevik faction as virtually an independent party openly rivaling the mensheviks in trying to obtain funds, gain control over the labor movement, establish a press, and set up an underground organization within the Russian empire. The milestone of autonomous organization was the party Conference of Prague, in 1912, which was a purely bolshevik undertaking, the only outsiders being police spies who at that time had succeeded in infiltrating even Lenin's Central Committee.

The years between 1905 and 1917 were, on the whole,

difficult for the entire Marxist movement in Russia. We have mentioned the intrigues and nasty disputes which racked its ranks and the police spies who managed to penetrate into its innermost councils. These were, moreover, years of defeat. The revolution had failed; reaction reigned supreme. Many Russian intellectuals were disillusioned with revolutionary activity, and many veteran fighters left the movement forever. The party was reduced to very small size, and it was in financial trouble. Its leaders were in exile abroad or in Siberian banishment. The working-class movement, as a thing apart from the party, was declining. Strikes and other workers' activities began to increase only around 1912, and many communist historians regard 1912 as a turning point in the history of their movement. But the major turning point in the history of bolshevism was the outbreak of the first World War. For the gap between bolsheviks and mensheviks became unbridgeable as a result of differences over the party's attitude toward the war.[3]

The outbreak of hostilities had shown that Marxist dogmas or hopes concerning international proletarian solidarity had been little more than a phrase and that national loyalties were stronger than class consciousness. Most working-class leaders, albeit with some reluctance, supported their countries' war effort. Lenin nevertheless urged the working class to turn their military weapons against their own ruling classes, fraternize with their fellow workers across the trenches, and turn the war into a world revolution. During the war, while living in Switzerland, he tried to rally like-minded comrades around him, organized conferences for the purpose, swore undying enmity to all those Marxists who had supported the war, and made plans for founding a new international organization of all truly revolutionary parties. The handful of men and women who came to his support, together with those who had been with him since about 1909, formed the bulk of the bolshevik leadership when the revolution of 1917 broke out. Among the latter were men like Zinoviev. Kamenev, Rykov, and Stalin, while

Bukharin and Radek, for instance, belonged to a somewhat younger generation of men who rallied around
Lenin about the time of the outbreak of the war.

Lenin was joined in 1917 by a considerable number of
Marxists who had hitherto refused to be identified with
bolshevism but who now supported Lenin because they
were attracted by the uncompromising radicalism of his
stand. These people include Leon Trotsky and a large
number of brilliant leaders forming his entourage, who
had previously tried to conciliate bolsheviks and mensheviks, as well as some outright mensheviks, as, for instance, the future commissar for foreign affairs, G.V.
Chicherin. As a result of this influx of new blood into the
highest ranks of the party in 1917, party membership became more heterogeneous in outlook than ever before;
and, corresponding to this heterogeneity, the democratic
representative institutions of the party acquired greater
weight in decision making than they had ever had. Moreover, one of the newcomers, Trotsky, came close to rivaling Lenin as the leader of the bolsheviks, though he never
quite equaled him in authority. He was popular with the
rank and file and was better known to outsiders than anyone except Lenin; but the old-timers in the party tended
to regard him with suspicion and envy.[4]

During 1917, when the range of attitudes and policies
expressed by bolshevik leaders widened and leadership to
some extent diffused, some of the comrades-in-arms who
had stuck by Lenin most faithfully during the difficult
interrevolutionary years found themselves out of tune
with him. During the eight months between the fall of
tsarism and the bolshevik seizure of power, Lenin's attitude was marked by uncompromising radicalism. His policy was to endorse sweepingly the most radical demands
voiced by Russia's lower classes. He endorsed the peasants' demand for the immediate distribution of the landlords' estates. He came out in favor of giving the workers
control over the factories. He supported the cry of Russia's national minorities for national self-determination,
including even separation from the Russian state. And he

advocated measures to end the war immediately. Lenin's radicalism in 1917 implied uncompromising resistance to the caretaker government that had instituted itself in the spring. He demanded its replacement by a government of popular action committees (soviets) in which only the revolutionary parties were represented. Furthermore, he showed an absolute intolerance of revolutionaries who were satisfied with, or for any reason preferred, compromise.

In short, Lenin from the very beginning was unwilling to regard the overthrow of tsarism as an end in itself or even as a major achievement giving time to pause. Instead, he saw it as a mere beginning, a prologue to further revolutionary events, an opportunity for quick advances, and he was eager to get done with the further tasks as quickly as possible. In advancing such ideas, he was at first far ahead of most of his closest friends and associates. They were unprepared for, and frightened by, his sweeping program and sought to prevent or soften what they thought would be rash, adventurous actions. Some, like Stalin, rallied around Lenin after a while. Others became ever more alarmed. Their conflict with Lenin came to a head in October of 1917, when, from his Finnish hiding place, he bombarded the Central Committee with messages urging them to prepare an armed uprising at once with the aim of overthrowing the provisional government and establishing a Soviet regime. Two of his closest associates, Zinoviev and Kamenev, publicly dissociated themselves from such a course of action and were virtually read out of the party by Lenin. Yet they had done little more than express openly the doubts shared by many of their comrades.

Once the bolsheviks had seized power in the name of the Soviet (at that time they were in the majority in this body), the heterogeneity of party leadership and the prevalence of open debate within this group were intensified by the fact that the first few years of communist rule brought acute problems that no one had anticipated. Crises can unify the group they confront; but they can also have divisive effects; the grave problems faced by the party in the first few years of its rule did both.

At the root of the problems was the fact that the Communist Party had come to power with the firm expectation that this event would produce a world-wide chain reaction of proletarian revolutions; and this world revolution in turn would ensure the immediate advent of socialism even in Russia. We shall have more to say about these expectations in the following chapter. It took only a few months of Soviet rule to convince at least Lenin that these ideals were not going to be attained immediately. With the gradual ebbing of hopes for a general European revolution, his government was not only forced to think of its own preservation; it also had to postpone the Good Society as far as domestic measures were concerned. The grim fight for survival in the civil war which broke out in the summer of 1918 required the abandonment of democratic ideals and the imposition in their stead of strict military discipline; and the economic ruin following in its wake forced Lenin to take the most stringent measures to save his regime from collapse. Moreover, it dawned on the communist leaders that the vigor with which substantial portions of the lower-class population of Russia had fought for the revolution did not necessarily imply that they were in general on a high level of literacy, education, or productivity. On the contrary, the human material at the disposal of the party was on an abysmally low cultural level—hardly the basis for the ideal communist society.

Some of the repressive measures taken during the civil war were defended by many communists as attempts to create immediately the communist or socialist society. Each new measure of nationalization and centralization, each new tightening of controls, was praised as the harbinger of true socialism. But other members of the party saw in these steps a betrayal of the ideas for which they had fought, and Lenin had to impose every such measure against vigorous opposition from leading party members. The ideas of 1917 thus served both to justify the civil-war measures (known in the history books as "war communism") by stirring expectations of the immediate attainment of socialism and to criticize them as a violation of communist ideals. It appeared that Lenin's left-wing followers, who had been the most sanguine in their expectations in 1917, tended to be the most critical of war communism and simultaneously to harbor the greatest illusions about its results. In contrast, the old-time Leninists, who had resisted their leader in 1917, were less burdened with idealistic hopes and with squeamishness. Consequently, war communism did not present them with such acute ideological problems.[5]

Once the civil war was won, the party, in a sudden about-face, made substantial concessions to free enterprise and other capitalist features; and once again the membership was jolted and perturbed, and many of them retained serious misgivings about the new policies which they regarded as a retreat from socialist principles. These heated debates, in the course of which Lenin was outvoted more than once in the Central Committee, prompted him to curb dissent and discussion within the party by the measures described above and by such devices as control over recruitment, assignments, and other personnel policies. Because of these steps to silence dissenting members, the doubts arising over the concessions made after the end of the civil war remained unexpressed in the main while Lenin was still alive. But they were to erupt all the more forcefully when illness and death removed him from the scene and the curtain rose on a new act in the history of Russian communism.*

This sketch of the history of the Russian Communist Party can, of course, offer no more than a few highlights of an involved and complex development. In summary: The party grew up as a tightly organized and self-conscious faction within the Russian Social-Democratic Labor Party; it strove to gain full control over the Russian working-class movement with the aim of making its own policies prevail; and its leader did everything within his power to make it into an organization whose every move

* See Chapter 6.

was well under his own control, rejecting and casting out all persons and groups who refused to submit to such control.

After the revolution, the effort to convert the working-class movement into an efficient and tightly controlled political machine (in Russian: *apparat*) was extended to the international working-class movement. On the basis of plans Lenin had conceived during World War I, he created an international league of communist parties, the Third, or Communist, International, the by-laws of which were drafted so as to resemble closely those of the Russian party and to give control over membership and policies of all its constituent parties to Lenin and his Russian colleagues. The Communist International, with its numerous auxiliary organizations, thus quickly became a global extension of the Russian *apparat*.*

Yet when Lenin became ill, the problems of party policy, organization, and personnel were by no means solved. A number of fundamental differences in attitude divided the party along policy lines. The resulting formation of factions was complicated by personal antagonisms and friendships between different groups of leaders. Finally, the death of the leader, in whose hands most lines of control and command had been concentrated, brought out serious unresolved problems of party government and precipitated a deep and prolonged crisis within the party. We shall give a brief account of it in the next chapter.

* See Chapter 7.

6

Phases of Soviet Rule

The history of communism comprises not only the growth of the party but also the development of the state and the society over which that party has been ruling for more than four decades. Because Soviet Russia for many years was the only country under the rule of a Communist Party, all the world regarded her as an experiment in socialist government—and so did the communists themselves. Consequently, the history of Soviet Russia has become part of the heritage of communism everywhere. It is an experience which in some fashion all adherents of the movement share and which they take into consideration, willingly or not, whenever and wherever they map out governmental policies. In this introductory essay we can do no more than provide a brief outline of the main phases of Soviet rule in Russia.

The bolsheviks expected their revolution to result in a world-wide chain reaction of proletarian revolutions, which, they assumed, would ensure the birth of a global (or at least all-European) socialist commonwealth. The kind of socialist commonwealth Lenin envisaged is described in some detail in his unfinished *The State and Revolution*, which he wrote in the fall of 1917 and which echoed sentiments widespread in his party at that time. In it he visualized that the creation of a soviet state would at once lead to the expropriation of capitalists and landowners and therefore to the abolition of commodity production (i.e., production for the market). It would lead to classless society, in which the material wants of all could be fully satisfied. Since by working for the common good all members of society would be working directly for themselves, they would, Lenin foresaw, gladly give their energies for production; no longer would there be incentive problems. Moreover, the need for men to dominate or exploit other men would disappear, and hence institutions of coercion and government, such as armies, police forces, courts, and bureaucracies, would disappear. The people would manage their communal affairs spontaneously, directly, rationally. The administration of the industrial establishment, in turn, would be reduced to simple tasks of accounting and controlling, tasks so simple that they could be performed by anyone. Since these would be all the "governmental" tasks remaining to be done, any "female cook" could run the government; and administrative responsibilities could therefore be rotated among all.

These sanguine expectations held by the bolsheviks in the last months of 1917 were not merely propaganda designed to justify their seizure of power. On the contrary, the bolsheviks were convinced that this ideal society was within reach, and it took some of them years to shed such beliefs. Since then, the blueprint Lenin provided for a classless and stateless society has become a source of embarrassment to the party, a symbol of unfulfilled dreams or broken promises, an idealistic mirror that mocked the face of an exceedingly drab reality.*

* Although Lenin's book on *The State and Revolution* is often assigned to students to acquaint them with the writings of Lenin, I should like to stress its unrepresentative nature. I should go so far as to say that it is the most unrepresentative,

For developments took a different turn. The workers of the West did not take up the cue tossed them by the Russian Revolution. The bolshevik regime of Russia remained isolated and harassed. Within the country, a protracted and bitter civil war broke out, and in the narrow territory remaining under Soviet rule uncooperative, hostile elements abounded. The regime truly had its back to the wall. It won the civil war partly because substantial sections of the peasantry and the national minorities joined the workers in supporting the regime actively or passively, or at least showed themselves more hostile to the counter-revolutionary forces than to the Red Army, and partly because the bolsheviks adopted stringent emergency measures to keep themselves in power. They imposed the strictest military discipline on the entire population, including their own supporters and party members. Like commandants of a besieged fortress, they commandeered every ounce of available human and material resources for the civil-war effort, disdaining neither to rob the peasant of his produce by force nor to employ tsarist officers, capitalist entrepreneurs, and other "bourgeois specialists." Ruling by stark terror, with the support at times of ignorant and dissolute mobs who often abused the power so suddenly thrust upon them, smashing existing institutions and assigning loyal revolutionaries to administrative jobs for which they were altogether unprepared, improvising and fumbling, they yet found this to be the time for brave cultural experiments in many fields, most of them based on the notion that the brotherhood of all men was about to become reality. Antagonizing countless supporters, they yet managed to inspire an entire generation of Russian youngsters with heaven-storming enthusiasm, with the readiness to sacrifice everything to the building of a world without exploitation and inequality, a socialist commonwealth that would begin as soon as the civil war

the most untypical work of all that Lenin has produced; it is an aberration from his customary thought pattern. See Robert V. Daniels, "The State and Revolution: A Case Study in the Genesis and Transformation of Communist Ideology," in *The American Slavic and East European Review*, XII, 22–43.

would be won. This was the heroic period of the Russian Revolution, usually referred to as the period of war communism, a period in which all the worst fears of antirevolutionary men in Russia and in the West were confirmed by the excesses of the Red Terror, the insolence of drunken or ragged proletarians, and the muddle of communist bureaucracy, while the image which Soviet Russia presented to her sympathizers abroad was still one of unsullied revolutionary pioneering.

Yet the ruthlessness of the civil-war emergency measures exhausted the credit of the bolshevik regime among many of its supporters. By the time the civil war was won, the regime was therefore close to political collapse. In addition, seven years of foreign and civil war had brought unspeakable economic ruin to the country. Drastic measures were required to restore the economy and pacify at least parts of the population. The measures adopted for the purpose are known as the New Economic Policy, or NEP. They consisted in the reintroduction of private enterprise in agriculture, trade, crafts, and small manufacture, with only foreign trade, major industries, and political rule remaining firmly in the hands of the party and its government. (Concessions made to Western business firms allowing them to exploit Soviet resources or build up manufacturing enterprises made no serious dent in these monopolies.)

The NEP meant a relaxation of bolshevik terror. Members of the old ruling classes remained disfranchised and discriminated against; but they were at least permitted to make a living. Workers still enjoyed privileges over the members of other classes, but economically the NEP benefited well-to-do peasants and small businessmen. Bold experiments were still conducted by the party in various cultural fields; but other currents in art, literature, science, and mores were at least tolerated. To the average Soviet citizen looking back to this period in the 1930's or 1940's, the years of the NEP must have appeared like a veritable golden age. After the hardships of the heroic period, normalcy seemed to have returned.

Yet this normalcy did not look attractive to many members of the Communist Party. To be sure, they had adopted the NEP as a necessary retreat; they had said, with Lenin, that they were accepting it "seriously and for a long time"; but nonetheless not all had accepted it gladly. True, most party members had had enough of civil war, terror, and heroism for a while. But not all were comfortable in the humdrum tasks of gradual economic reconstruction and of teaching illiterates the ABC or with the patient tolerance shown to peasants, small businessmen, and foreign concessionaires. The men at the head of the party had spent their lives in an agonizing struggle for a lofty goal. Most of them could not possibly be satisfied unless there was a chance to make that goal—socialism—reality.

Conflicting schools of thought developed within the Russian Communist Party concerning the manner in which socialism might be made to come about. One group, usually considered to be the right wing of the party, developed an almost Fabian theory of inevitable gradualness, based on thoughts expressed in Lenin's last articles and speeches. They held that the uneasy compromise between socialism and free enterprise would give way to pure socialism in the course of a slow, organic evolution and that in similar fashion the social basis of the regime, that is, the "alliance" between workers and peasants, would gradually "grow over" into a purely proletarian society. The economic transformation, entailing the gradual waning of free enterprise and other capitalist features, would come about as the result of free competition between capitalism and socialism, and not through coercion or governmental arbitrariness. The most outspoken among them therefore argued that the free-enterprise features of the NEP ought to be fostered and encouraged rather than curbed. Precisely the free unfolding of capitalism—perhaps with constitutional democracy added—would hasten the growth of socialism. The party's chief role in this process, they tended to think, was that of promoting the cultural revolution, that is, the transformation, by education, of Russia's ignorant, backward masses into informed, sophisticated, responsible citizens. The cultural revolution, they thought, was the most essential prerequisite and the surest guarantee of the eventual victory of socialism over capitalism.

The people who developed gradualist views were of different types. The chief theoreticians of gradualism appear to have been antitotalitarian idealists such as N. N. Bukharin who in the period of war communism (if not before) had become suspicious of violent and authoritarian methods. In their attempts to provide their political views with ideological support, they interpreted Marxism in strictly determinist fashion, leading to the conclusion that it is impossible to go against economic laws or to skip historically predetermined stages of development, and that it would be foolish or criminal to attempt it. Similarly, Marxist dialectics was transformed by Bukharin into a theory of equilibrium which supported his reluctance to engage in daring and radical political experiments. Theoreticians such as he were supported by a host of party bureaucrats who seemed loath to jeopardize the interests of their political machine for the sake of bold new adventures, people whose vested interest in the existing system made them timid if not conservative.[1]

Against the gradualists stood those Party leaders who argued that the NEP was a danger which must be overcome by daring measures. It was a political danger because the dominating position taken in the national economy by the successful peasant and small businessman sooner or later would be transformed into political dominance, so that the proletarian regime was in danger of being swamped by the petty bourgeoisie. Economically the NEP was dangerous, they held, because Soviet Russia was threatened with the prospect of getting stuck in economic backwardness. Socialism, they argued, was possible only in a modern industrial society; and the first task of the communist regime would therefore have to be to erect a modern industrial structure.

The spokesmen for the left wing of the Russian

Communist Party—outstanding among them were Leon Trotsky and Eugene Preobrazhenski—gave dramatic emphasis to their theory by calling for a policy of *primitive* (or *primary*) *socialist accumulation*. Primary accumulation, in Marxist theory, is that sanguinary process of robbery, piracy, conquest, extortion, and other violent means through which society accumulates the material resources and "free" labor that enable the capitalist mode of production to develop. In the words of Marx, it is "an accumulation not the result of the capitalist mode of production, but its starting point"; and he adds that it "plays in Political Economy about the same part as original sin in theology." [2] Marx describes it with loathing and moral indignation, concluding that capitalism comes into the world "dripping from head to foot, from every pore, with blood and dirt." [3] This then was the image Trotsky and Preobrazhenski evoked in demanding a policy of primitive socialist accumulation. They argued that just as capitalism could arise only after surplus wealth and a surplus population had been accumulated, so the creation of an industrial base was the essential prerequisite for building socialism. In addition, industrialization was the only policy that could prevent the revolution from being overwhelmed by peasants and NEP men (small businessmen). They warned that the policy they were advocating would require harsh measures and dictatorial discipline. The resources to be invested in industrialization would have to be provided by Russia's population through forced savings. And yet they argued that the task could be accomplished without living standards falling drastically and without a renewal of the Red Terror of civil-war days. Whatever the measures and the methods, however, the revolution would be lost if it did not industrialize.

On the very left wing of the party, there were small groups of leaders who argued that the revolution had already been lost or betrayed, that it had followed a cycle similar to that of the French Revolution, in which the radical Jacobin dreams of equality and justice had been destroyed by the Thermidorian reaction and the ensuing

Bonapartist dictatorship. According to such men as Shliapnikov and Sapronov, leaders of the ultraleftist opposition, the ideals of 1917 had been betrayed by the Communist Party itself. Instead of socialism, a mixture of capitalist free enterprise and industrial dictatorship had been set up, they argued; instead of proletarian rule, rule by the party, and not even the entire party at that, but only the handful of leaders constituting the core of the Old Guard. These men, ardently committed to the anarcho-syndicalist dreams of 1917, ultimately came to the conclusion that a third revolution (third after the two revolutions of February and October of 1917) was needed, this one to be a genuine proletarian revolution to overthrow the dictatorship of the party and to establish a genuine socialist workers' democracy.

As we shall see, these divergent views concerning the most desirable or necessary development of the Russian revolution were linked with equally conflicting policy lines concerning the policies of the international communist movement. Disputes over policy and ultimate goals, moreover, led to discussions in virtually every other field of learning, thought, and action; and the 1920's, more than any other period, therefore witnessed a thorough and highly controversial reëxamination of Marxism and Leninism in all its details, a debate that was far more open than any similar disputes within the party were later allowed to be.

The differences of opinion over the further development of the revolution began to plague the party soon after the beginning of the NEP. They were quite heated in the last year of Lenin's life and became extremely bitter after his death, which added the fuel of an intense power struggle to the fire of ideological arguments. Not only opinions but personalities and ambitions, too, clashed head-on, and the conflict split the party into hardly reconcilable factions. By "party" we mean that small group of Old Guard leaders who as members of its highest policy-making and administrative bodies were in actual command of the party. Even before Lenin was dead, maneuvering began in this high command to settle the succession problem. Interest centered on the role and personality of Trotsky, who in the minds of many people outside and inside the party was the heir apparent. Although he had for many years opposed Lenin and his bolshevik faction and joined them only in the summer of 1917, it was he who had been the chief tactician of the bolshevik seizure of power, creator of the Red Army and main strategist of the civil war, savior of Leningrad, and second in prestige only to Lenin himself. Abroad, it was customary to mention Lenin and Trotsky in the same breath as the two-man team ruling Soviet Russia. Within the party, however, there were many leaders who well remembered Trotsky's ancient conflicts with the bolsheviks and the comparatively recent vintage of his party membership. To be sure, in joining he had brought with him a bevy of friends who at once became prominent leaders under Lenin and could support Trotsky from positions of strength within the party. But against this faithful cohort stood a broad stratum of old associates of the dead leader who deeply resented the newcomer's prestige and power. Trotsky's own personality was not designed to help him win his colleagues' favor. The brilliance of his mind, his pen, and his oratory was matched by great arrogance and tactlessness, by a certain inability to deal with people and to recognize political constellations within the party. As a political manipulator he was no match for the old Leninist organizers. Finally, as architect of the Red Army he could easily be regarded as or alleged to be a potential Bonaparte, who would pervert the revolution while saving it and make himself the dictator; and anything Trotsky might have done to defend himself against this suspicion would only have increased it. Seeing this, he did nothing to cleanse himself of the Bonapartist taint. On the contrary, there is some evidence that he regarded himself as Lenin's legitimate heir and promoted his candidacy for the position of party chief, aided by some of his followers in the party's high ranks. These moves evoked a systematic propaganda campaign in which the old Leninists, headed by G. E.

Zinoviev, Lenin's old-time companion and faithful shadow, tried to stigmatize Trotsky as a menshevik. After these ideological preparations, Trotsky and those loyal to him were demoted and isolated; and, while he was not denied access to the centers of decision making (he remained in the Politburo until October 1926 and in the Central Committee for a year after that), his vote in these organizations struck against a solid wall of hostility. Meanwhile, the policy-making power of the party's administrative organs, from which Trotsky and his followers were excluded, grew apace.

The next phase was a fight among the victors in the struggle against Trotsky, especially between Zinoviev (joined by another old comrade of Lenin's, L. B. Kamenev) and the party's general secretary, J. V. Stalin. Zinoviev's political strength was considerable. As chairman of the Executive Committee of the Communist International, he was the world's number-one communist. In addition to being a member of the Politburo, he was also boss of the important Leningrad regional party organization, while the Moscow organization was Kamenev's stronghold. In their fight against the General Secretary, these two former associates of his tried to pit the power, prestige, and the votes of their satrapies against Stalin's growing control over the total party machinery. This attempt was made at the fourteenth Party Congress, the last congress to have exhaustive open debates (December 1925). The attempt failed. The so-called Leningrad opposition was voted down, and Zinoviev, Kamenev, and their supporters were removed from positions of authority and power.

This defeat was followed by a last-ditch effort in which Trotsky, Zinoviev, and their associates joined forces in a desperate attempt to regain their strength and influence in the party and to overthrow the party regime that had become entrenched. The Trotsky-Zinoviev opposition was a heterogeneous alliance of groups and personalities, which comprised old Leninists as well as the most prominent among those leaders who, like Trotsky, had joined Lenin in 1917; authoritarian and democratic bolsheviks;

hard Marxists and soft Marxists; theoreticians and organization men. The bitter struggle which ensued between them and the Stalin faction (in which Bukharin was the outstanding theoretician) lasted for about six months in 1927 and rocked the party dangerously. Its outcome, Stalin's complete victory, was probably inevitable, because the whole strength of the party organization was in the hands of the general secretary, who wielded it with considerable skill and cunning. Many historians date his dictatorship from the days of his victory over the Trotsky-Zinoviev opposition, and indeed his strength had now become unassailable. To be sure, while the rank and file membership of the party had been reduced to obedient yes men and while secretaries and administrators loyal to Stalin ran local and regional party organizations with an iron hand, the Central Committee, the Politburo, and other central party organizations still retained genuine decision-making power. But even there, Stalin could usually be certain of dependable majorities.

Once Stalin was well in control of the party, he adopted a great deal of the program of his left-wing critics—and as a consequence faced new opposition, this time from theoreticians like Bukharin and organization men like Tomsky and Rykov, who for various reasons were firmly committed to a program of caution and slow reform. This opposition fared little better than previous ones; within a comparatively brief period, its leaders were eliminated from positions of influence. Acknowledging that economic as well as political stagnation were major dangers facing the Soviet regime, Stalin now launched a program of rapid industrialization on the basis of a five-year plan —the most ambitious, not to say reckless, of the various plans elaborated by the party economists. Stalin himself later referred to the years of this first five-year plan as another revolution (adding that it was a revolution made from above); and rightly so, because not only did the five-year plans achieve revolutionary changes in the economic, social, political, and cultural fabric of Russia but these changes were initiated in truly revolutionary frenzy,

which gripped the party and imparted its spirit to all fields
of endeavor.

The plan for industrialization was carried out with utter disregard for considerations of economic balance or
rationality, or for the demands of the consumer. Instead,
it was executed as a desperate crash program. The Russian
population again suffered lean years, with a drastic low-
ering of living standards, as every ounce of available energy—human as well as material—was pressed into service and pumped into investment. In agriculture, the new
revolution brought with it a virtual civil war against the
peasantry. The regime wanted to neutralize the peasants
once and forever as a potential political force, wanted to
subject them to economic, political, and cultural controls
and pressures, and particularly wished to make sure that
every year's harvest would reach the hungry mouths of
the city dwellers. For without food and agricultural raw
materials, the industrialization effort would be doomed.
To secure these ends, the party decided to abolish private
enterprise in farming and force the peasants into cooperative, or collective, farms, where they would be subject to
all these controls, primarily because collective farms would
not own the essential means of production—tractors and
implements—but would have to rent them from government pools. Motor and repair shops were therefore in a
position of control and could become centers not only for
the economic exploitation of the farmers but also for their
political control and education and for efforts to urbanize
the farm population.

Peasant resistance to the attempt to "collectivize" them
was bitter and persistent, and the regime succeeded in
overcoming it only through a virtual civil war, in which
hundreds of thousands of peasants lost their lives, millions
were rendered destitute, and the agricultural economy
of the Soviet Union suffered damages that were not re-
paired until more than twenty years later. In the wake of
collectivization, a disastrous famine killed millions of
Soviet citizens.

For the first few years the industrialization was accompanied by a new radicalism in cultural and educational affairs, a new stress on proletarian exclusiveness, but in other aspects Soviet Russia moved further away from socialist goals and methods. The workers, whose trade unions during the NEP had retained at least a modicum of bargaining and administrative power, were totally subjected to discipline under a new managerial system. Where formerly Russia's government and industry had been managed "collectively," that is, through administrative committees, a command principle was now instituted, whereby all agencies were to be run by single managers with full authority and responsibility. The country's administration was thus streamlined to resemble the organization and management of giant corporations in the Western world —a process through which the party itself had already gone some years before.

Two additional developments were required before Soviet Russia was transformed into the type of society it is today. I shall call one of these the cultural counterrevolution. The other one is known as the Great Purge. The two phenomena are closely related to each other.

The origins and meaning of the Great Purge remain a matter of conjecture and controversy. The paranoid and vengeful personality of Stalin is as unsatisfactory an explanation as the totalitarian pattern of Soviet rule with its presumed need for an occasional personnel turnover through the means of a bloody housecleaning. We must take into consideration the tremendous difficulties faced by Stalin's regime in the 1930's. The reckless pace of industrialization and collectivization had led to serious bottlenecks and deficiencies in the national economy. In the party, the government, and the economy, serious morale problems were created by the arbitrariness with which impossible tasks were imposed on ill-trained personnel or inadequate facilities. In international affairs the Soviet Union began to face new grave threats from strong neighbors to the west and the east. It is plausible to assume that the victims of the Great Purge served, among other things, as scapegoats on whom all blame for these failures could be heaped. Furthermore, numerous party members may have been in a state of genuine panic and therefore quite receptive to what was alleged to be evidence of sabotage, treason, and the like.

Whatever the reasons, the fact is that between 1935 and 1938 the USSR became the stage for a veritable orgy of police activity, in which the party, the government apparatus, the economy, the armed forces, the schools and universities, and all the professions were decimated, especially in their higher ranks, from which vast numbers of personnel disappeared into the labor camps or execution dungeons of the secret police. In the Communist Party, nearly everyone who had ever disagreed with the dictator was physically eliminated; and the same fate befell countless officials within the party and outside of it who were denounced for, or suspected of, harboring dissent. As a result, the administrative body of Soviet society was decapitated; an entire generation of leaders fell victims to the purge and an entire generation of younger ones moved up to fill their places. Furthermore, we might say that the purge destroyed the Communist Party, although I know of no one who has expressed this fact so drastically. Nonetheless I believe it to be true. Not only did the Great Purge kill off or jail almost all those who had been members of the party before and during the revolution of 1917. In that sense, the party of Lenin certainly was destroyed. But in addition the place and function which the party had had in Soviet society was changed so drastically that we might speak of its destruction. In the first two decades of the Russian Revolution, the party had been the sovereign of the Soviet Union, to use an old-fashioned term. It had been in charge. It had acted as if it owned the country or as if it were administering it in the name of the working class. This undisputed sovereignty of the party was replaced, in the Great Purge, by the undisputed sovereignty of Josef Stalin. He made use of the party as one of the instruments of his rule; but he used it no more, and in practice assigned no greater importance to it, than the government administration or the

political police. To be precise, Stalin's central organ of
rule was his personal secretariat, which, even though it
had close connections with the party and the police, was
yet apart from them and above them, assigning them a
secondary role.*

The cultural counterrevolution, or, as Timasheff called
it, the Great Retreat, was a process of transformation
consummated about the time of the Great Purge. Its outward manifestation was a decided return to traditionalism
in education, art, social science, mores, and other elements that make up a society's cultural life. It included
such developments as the reintroduction of military ranks
and tsarist-style uniforms, the strengthening of the family and of the authority of both parents and teachers, and
the abandonment of *avant-garde* art styles in favor of the
naïve naturalism of what Hitler called "heroic art" and
which in the USSR is called "socialist realism."

But if this was a *return* to traditionalism, from where
did it return? The answer is, from Marxism. True, Marxism remained as the acknowledged creed of the Soviet
state, hailed as the last word in social and natural science
as well as philosophy, elevated to the status of official
dogma. But only the words of Marx became dogma; essential elements of what he meant and what he wanted
were abandoned. In returning to traditionalism in cultural
and intellectual life, the Soviet regime rejected at least two
major elements of Marxism. One was the dream of a society without alienation or (to eschew utopianism) without
that surplus alienation which goes beyond the minimum
of alienation required to keep a modern industrial economy operating,[4] a dream which had been kept very much
alive in the period of the NEP and the first five-year plan.
The regime that emerged in the mid-1930's seems to have

* We might recognize the justification for asserting that the
party was destroyed in the following figures of the proportion
of voting delegates at party congresses who were party members before 1921, that is, before the end of the civil war:

Seventeenth Congress (1934) . . . . 80.0 per cent
Eighteenth Congress (1939) . . . . 19.4 per cent

come to the conclusion that the yearning for such a society, for the institutions and processes depicted in Lenin's *The State and Revolution,* would never, or not for a very long time, be satisfied, and that the yearning itself, therefore, was disturbing and disruptive. So it became subversive to talk about or ask for the withering away of the state, the disappearance of oppressive institutions and social or economic inequality. At the same time, Marxist doctrines or words were twisted in such a fashion as to create the impression that a major portion of the dreams of Marx and Engels had indeed come true. Socialism had been achieved. The class struggle had been abolished. The Soviet people were a happy people.

The assertion that socialism had been achieved implied the rejection of one other element of Marxism, namely, the use of social science for the purpose of analyzing social phenomena as the superstructure of exploitative economic systems. Marxism had not been only a dream of the future. It had also been critical of the past and the present; and it is by its very method and orientation a critical social theory. Soviet society, however, continued to incorporate intense alienation and superalienation of all its citizens, which the Soviet Union became altogether unwilling to admit. Soviet theory has been reluctant to concede that its own society incorporates repression, domination, alienation, and exploitation. At most, it hints at remaining differences between the interests of the state and those of the individual. Being unwilling to admit these repressive features, it cannot, of course, justify them, as well it might be able to do. As a matter of fact, we might say that one of the main distinguishing features of Stalinist theory is this unwillingness to admit the necessity (in bolshevik terms) for repressive measures. Stalin and his comrades obviously did not dare take the people into their confidence about the hard road that lay ahead in the drive for rapid industrialization. I think that here lies the main difference between Stalin and Trotsky: the policies they advocated were similar; but the latter was honest about their harshness, whereas Stalinism seeks to conceal it behind phrases to the effect that the Soviet world is the best of all possible worlds. Important among the ideological taboos resulting from this unwillingness to look reality in the face is the inability to admit that the isolation of the "proletarian" revolution in a backward peasant country was, from the point of view of original Marxism, a historical freak and, from the point of view of the proletarian world revolution, an unmitigated disaster. There is therefore even a marked reluctance to admit that tsarist Russia was a backward society in comparison with Western Europe. These ideological taboos have little to do with Marxism; on the contrary, they are in sharp contradiction to it. Marxist theory, in fact, has been thoroughly emasculated and converted into apologetics. Today, even though Marx and Engels are the prophets of Soviet society, their writings are available to Soviet readers only in expurgated editions; their earlier works particularly are either suppressed or explained away, for these works contain in the clearest form their critique of domination and their yearning for liberty. Entire concepts have been eliminated from the storehouse of Marxist methods, because they might yield conclusions uncomfortable to the regime. Occasionally, Stalin even ventured to criticize some of their works openly; for instance, he denounced Engels for his hatred of tsarist Russia and his eagerness to see Western Europe united in a war to destroy that hated state.

The turn to traditionalism came to pervade all of Soviet culture. In the teaching of history, the preoccupation with class wars and economic developments and with the depressing features of tsarist Russia's past gave way to the old-fashioned kings-and-battles approach familiar to us from our own high-school texts; and the heroes no longer were the exploited masses but Russian emperors, generals, and conquerors of backward people in the Caucasus and Central Asia. Art turned into a weapon of mass propaganda, using the vehicle of popular style and expressing ideas designed to give cheer to the laboring masses. The idea of equality, which had inspired many of

the deeds of the revolution and the civil war, now was
denounced as a petty-bourgeois delusion; and henceforth
in thought and in fact Soviet society came to lay stress on
social differences, for the avowed purpose of providing incentives that had previously been considered unnecessary.
By emphasizing differences of salary and rank, peak performance was encouraged, so that the Soviet population
came under the sway of what Marcuse has called the
"performance principle." To back up the system of rewards, police terror and concentration camps were provided, imposing stern sanctions on anyone not conforming to the regime's demands. Finally, as we have seen, a
social theory was carefully designed not to unmask inequalities and alienation but to conceal them. Malfunc-
tions, henceforth, were explained not as the symptoms of
an ill social system (as Marx and Engels would have
done) but as moral failings of individuals who were either
weak and therefore had to be treated sternly or who were
criminal conspirators who had to be eliminated. Or mal-
functions were explained as unavoidable mechanical difficulties; for instance, Soviet medical theory recognizes
almost no other cause of insanity but physiological deficiencies of the brain. In all these and many other fields,
Soviet culture returned to the Victorian age.

With these developments, Soviet life was set for the
next two decades; and, after discussing the development
of international communism in the first twenty-five years
after the revolution, we shall try to sketch the pattern
of Soviet communism during these two decades.

7

The Communist
International, 1919–1943

When the Russian bolsheviks seized power in 1917, they firmly expected that their deed would spark proletarian revolutions in the advanced countries of Western Europe. As a matter of fact, most of them thought that without world-wide revolution the establishment of a communist regime in a country like Russia made no sense whatever. Socialism, in their minds, presupposed a high stage of industrial development and a numerous, politically mature working class that could use this industrial establishment in rational fashion so as to ensure material plenty for all. In any society not coming up to these conditions, the erection of a socialist government was thought to be a premature and dangerous adventure. Either the socialist party would be overthrown very quickly, running the risk of total annihilation by the victorious counter-revolution; or, if against all odds it maintained itself in power, it could do so only by catering to the interests of a population not yet receptive to a Marxist program; the proletarian regime would turn into a sad caricature of it-self and greatly discredit the whole Marxist movement.

And yet the bolsheviks seized power. Compelled by the traditions of their own movement to do nothing that did not correspond to Marxist prognoses or could not be fitted into Marxist programs of action, their leaders had to as-sume that the world revolution was around the corner and that the productive potential of a socialist Europe would secure the gains made by the revolution in Russia. Not all bolshevik leaders shared this confidence—those who did not hotly argued against seizing power—but those who did must not be regarded necessarily as utopian dreamers or reckless adventurers. On the contrary, there were many indications in 1917 that Europe was on the brink of revolution. A disastrous war had ruined her econ-omies and shaken her regimes. Troops in France, Italy, and Germany had mutinied. Grave political unrest had made itself felt despite wartime censorship and emergency military rule. Where such indications were absent, their own theory told the men around Lenin that a revolution *had* to be in the making as a result of the war. And that this would be a proletarian revolution ushering in social-ism, they all took for granted, just as Marx and Engels on the eve of 1848 had taken for granted that the coming revolution would inevitably be transformed into a prole-tarian one.

The bolshevik hopes were disappointed. The Russian Revolution remained isolated and, only a few months after the October uprising, had to adjust to the disappointing need for coexistence with capitalism by signing a peace treaty with Imperial Germany. To be sure, in signing this document, Lenin and his associates thought that they were only buying time sufficient for the world revolution to catch its breath. But the short breather extended to decades, and the very same arguments which had ration-alized coexistence for but a little while came to sanction it for a long period. Rationalizing coexistence, however, meant rationalizing the pursuit of a policy devised for the purpose of securing the survival of the Soviet state. Co-existence therefore meant the emergence of a Soviet national interest or *raison d'état,* the pursuit of which was said to coincide with the interests of the proletarian world revolution.[1]

Still, by opting for coexistence, the Russian communists had not meant to abandon the cause of the world revolution. On the contrary, they signed their peace treaty with a capitalist power only so that the revolution might be given a chance to get under way. The war was still going on, after all, and in their eyes the world was still on the very brink of proletarian revolution. And indeed, even when the military conflict ended in November of 1918, the vehement economic, social, and political disturbances ensuing in the wake of the war lasted for another five years, keeping alive the most ambitious communist hopes.

During the war, Lenin had demanded that a new International be formed to replace the Second International, that world-wide federation of socialist parties which the war had destroyed. He had been exasperated by the leaders of these parties when with little hesitation they decided to support the war effort of their governments and thereby showed that national loyalty was stronger than their feeling of solidarity with the proletarians of all countries. In Lenin's eyes, they were traitors to the cause of the proletarian revolution, and he was determined not to be associated with them any longer. A revival of an international organization of working-class parties there must be, but definitely without any of the leaders who in his opinion had no place in, and could not contribute anything to, the party of the international proletariat. There were many socialist leaders who like Lenin regretted the collapse of international working-class solidarity and who joined him in criticizing the leaders of the European socialist parties; and yet many of them were hesitant to perpetuate the gulf that had opened between revolutionaries and moderates. Instead, they were eager to repair solidarity by trying to resurrect the international organization that had crumbled in 1914. Lenin's scorn of these people was as vehement as his hatred of the moderates.

Early in 1919 a congress of radical socialists assembled in Moscow to create the new International Lenin had demanded. The time seemed propitious. True, the Spartacus uprising in Germany had just been drowned in blood. But Hungary and Bavaria were in the hands of communist governments. Revolts against Western rule seemed to be brewing in the Near and Far East. All of Europe was in the throes of a violent postwar crisis. Still, the parties or factions represented, or purporting to be represented, at the founding congress were as yet without substantial following or even organization. Some delegates were extremely hesitant to help create an international socialist organization designed for the express purpose of keeping out the majority of socialist leaders and organizations. They would have preferred a renewal of the old International. But Lenin was eager to go ahead precisely because he wanted to anticipate and forestall the revival of the Second International. He wanted to face international socialism with a *fait accompli* and thus force all socialists to take sides, either with the new international or against it. The statutes of the new organization, adopted by the Second Congress, in 1920, were designed to enforce this compulsion to choose by imposing conditions on every would-be member party designed to antagonize and eliminate all those desiring a compromise—the famous twenty-one conditions. In addition, these statutes had the effect of imposing Lenin's principles of organization on every member party and on the Third International as a whole. Moreover, since that organization was designed to facilitate the exercise of leadership or command over a disciplined political machine, the imposition of Leninist organization also spelled the imposition of Leninist (or Russian) policies on the Third International, since quite naturally the Russian communists, with their prestige as successful revolutionaries, dominated the top command of the International from the very beginning. The many

communist parties which came into life after the creation
of the International, and also the even more numerous
auxiliary organizations in all the world, in this fashion
became appendages of the Russian *apparat,* in organization as well as in policy.

From its very beginning up to its dissolution, the policies of the Communist International were confused by the
ambiguity of its main aims. Ostensibly, its objective was to
promote proletarian revolution everywhere and, as an
auxiliary move, to promote colonial revolutions in areas
dominated by Western powers. But the pursuit of this goal
was complicated by the fact that all communist parties
were also expected to support the national interests of the
USSR; and these interests were not always easy to recon-
cile with the presumed interests of revolution making. In
fact, the evidence strongly suggests that, at least in
Europe, where the USSR tried very hard to coexist with
the leading capitalist nations, the efforts of the Communist International and those of the Soviet Commissariat
for Foreign Affairs eternally embarrassed and frustrated
and negated each other. Western communists could not
but be aware of the baneful influence of Soviet national
interests over the policies of their parties. Nor were they
entirely happy that Russia was the country which became
the pathbreaker and model for the development of a proletarian revolution. This raw and uncouth land of illiterate peasants, governed with a mixture of inefficiency and
oriental ruthlessness that repelled many visitors, was not
really a very suitable advertising sign for Marxist communism—certainly not in the first two or three decades of
its existence. On the contrary, it was in many ways a
source of embarrassment for Western communists. Meanwhile, Western diplomats and bourgeois politicians, compelled by various reasons to seek friendly relations with
the Soviet Union, could not, in their turn, help being
aware (even if they had not been reminded constantly by
their constituents) that Moscow was not only the capital of a state with which it was necessary to coexist but
also the headquarters and planning center of an interna-

tional revolutionary movement aiming at the overthrow
of all bourgeois governments.

In Asia, the incompatibility between Soviet foreign policy and the activities of the Communist International was
not nearly so pronounced. In China, Afghanistan, Persia,
and Turkey, Moscow was dealing with revolutionary regimes seeking to emancipate their countries from Western
domination. Colonial revolution could be fitted into the
policies of Soviet foreign relations as well as into the policies of world communism. And yet, on closer examina-
tion, difficulties abounded in this area of the world too.
While communist theory sought to convert the colonial
revolution into an ally and an auxiliary force of the Western proletarian revolution, strategies to promote this end
had not been elaborated and were a matter of keen controversy. Questions concerning the aims that ought to be
promoted in colonial revolutions and the objectives that
ought to be set, the forces with which communist parties
ought to, or might, ally themselves, the nature of such alliances and the very meaningfulness of communist parties
in countries where no industrial proletariat existed—these
and many similar problems faced the strategists of the Communist International. Many different methods were tried:
occasional attempts to spread communism by force of arms;
the founding of communist parties, which then sought
a mass basis among the urban workers, the peasants, or
even national and religious minorities, and which were
ever prone to be dismayed by Moscow's orders to ally
themselves with other revolutionary parties. Furthermore,
in order to aid the colonial revolution, Moscow (and it is
not always clear whether Asian policy emanated from the
International or from the Soviet Foreign Office) at times
supported popular revolutionary parties or leaders (such
as the Kuo Min Tang or Kemal), anti-Western princes
(such as Reza Pahlevi in Iran and Amanullah Khan in
Afghanistan), or even feudal lords like Ibn Saud, as long
as they were actively opposing the West (meaning especially Britain). Here too, therefore, considerations of for-

eign policy and revolution making came into conflict with each other, to the eventual detriment of both.

A further difficulty besetting the policies of the Comintern was the result of overcentralization. The International had been organized in the image of the Russian Communist Party not only because its kind of organization made it into a centralized, disciplined striking organization. That pattern of organization was rationalized further by the assumption that the working classes everywhere are basically alike. When Marx and Engels in the *Communist Manifesto* said that the proletarians have no fatherland, they presupposed an international solidarity of workers who in their living conditions and problems, their thinking and their political goals were more like each other than like the capitalists in their own countries. In short, Marx and Engels assumed that capitalism, fundamentally, was the same everywhere. Hence the possibility of an international, united proletarian movement. Lenin and his comrades subscribed to these views; and the Third International was organized so as to serve as the united, centralized Communist Party of all proletarians everywhere.

On a very high level of abstraction, the view of the workers of the world having certain problems and interests in common may have been defensible. But, concretely (and that means also politically), it was a mistake. The working class of each country could, rather, be expected to have problems of its own and to fight its own capitalists with weapons and strategies attuned to its own special conditions. If this is accepted, it will be clear that over-centralization and its corollary, the imposition of a unified policy line on the International, were a serious blunder which must have wrecked the chances of many a revolution.

The programs and strategies of the various member parties were thus fitted to the Procrustean bed of the Comintern's world-wide party line. Resistance to any of the more disastrous decisions which this procedure imposed on the various parties was stifled and punished as a serious breach of discipline. Communist parties were ill equipped, therefore, to accommodate leaders who thought for themselves or who thought that conditions in their own countries demanded a special course of action. The rapid turnover of leaders in the bolshevik party from its very beginnings therefore came to be a characteristic feature of the Communist International as well. The situation was not at all improved by the fact that disputes over policy were often intertwined with, or affected by, the struggle for power raging among the leaders. More specifically, conflicts within the Third International were closely tied to the bitter fights within the Russian party and were decided by the outcome of these fights, so that personnel turnover within the various member parties faithfully mirrored the personnel changes in the Russian party. In many ways, the cards were stacked against the Comintern's becoming an effective promoter of any rational policy.

After all I have said, it should not astonish anyone that the Third International was one gigantic failure. It did not succeed in creating a single proletarian dictatorship or communist regime. Nor did it manage to preserve and strengthen many of the strong communist parties that had been created in the years after World War I, although some of these parties survived World War II or even emerged from it more numerous and influential than ever before. Finally, the Comintern must be considered a dismal failure in its efforts to shield the Soviet Union and promote its national interests. I shall try to support these generalizations by a brief survey of the history of the International.

In the first years after World War I, valuable time was lost in gathering experience and organizing. The creation of the Comintern required vigorous efforts to persuade all like-minded socialist leaders to split off from the more moderate parties to which they had belonged and to found communist parties conforming in organization and policy to the Russian model. Some of the member parties started

out as small, insignificant sects. Others acquired a mass
following fairly quickly, especially the Communist Party
of Germany (KPD), which soon became and for some
years remained the center of the International's hopes.
The new parties were as yet unsure of their goals and
methods. In their sporadic attempts at promoting proletarian revolutions and seizing power they placed great reliance on organizers and leaders sent by Moscow, usually
Russian or Hungarian comrades whose experience in real
revolutions gave them tremendous prestige. Nonetheless,
the first attempts at revolution were handled in amateur-
ish fashion and ended in failure, as did the desperate attempt, made in 1920, at exporting revolution at bayonet
point by conquering Poland. In the wake of these failures
came not only the first purge of disobedient leaders but
also the first major switch in the policy line of the Communist International: after the abortive communist revolution in Germany in 1921, the International abandoned
such reckless adventures, decided that the major danger
to the working class movement lay in right-wing authoritarianism, and consequently adopted the policy of the
"United Front" with the moderate socialists. In line with
this policy, communist parties were enjoined to offer collaboration to moderate socialists, ostensibly for the purpose of safeguarding democratic institutions and workers'
rights, but in reality with the aim of infiltrating socialist
parties and more particularly trade unions. In China,
which together with Germany was the main focus of
Comintern hopes in these years, the new policy led to the
alliance and actual merger of the Chinese Communist
Party with the Kuo Min Tang—a step which at the time
was hailed with enthusiasm, though in the end it brought
only disaster to the Chinese communists.

In Europe the policy of the United Front came to
naught for several reasons. For one thing, the moderate
socialists were generally in no mood to ally themselves
with communist parties, especially since the communists
themselves were frank enough to admit their desire to destroy or swallow up the moderates. Secondly, as the after-

math of World War I came to a dramatic climax, it seems
that the rank-and-file membership of the communist parties became impatient with the moderate and cautious
defensive policy which the United Front implied. While
political and economic chaos engulfed Europe, the high
command of the International and the leaders of the
European parties were divided; and the top decision
makers hesitated. In the end, an attempt to unleash revolution in Germany, which was finally made in October of
1923, was bungled and ended in disaster. Changes of personnel and policy followed as a matter of course.[2]

Following the debacle of the "German October" in
1923, the Communist International settled down to the
serious work of consolidating its substantial gains in Western and Central Europe. It found it possible to elaborate
greatly its network of auxiliary organizations set up to
organize and educate different groups in the population
of the capitalist countries. A great deal of energy was
spent also in the recurrent fights against opposing factions
and, once the major oppositions had been eliminated, in
making personnel changes which brought to the top dis-
ciplinarians and obedient spokesmen of the Kremlin, organization men who could not be expected to make any
trouble. This change of personnel was called the "bol-
shevization" of the Comintern.

For serious revolution making, the time did not seem
propitious. In Europe and in the New World, this was a
period of "normalcy" and prosperity, which brought with
it a flowering of constitutional democracy and middle-
class culture. Sporadic outbursts of labor trouble, as for
instance the British General Strike of 1926, did not yield
any benefits to the communist parties. In Asia, national
revolutions continued to break out. But in India, China,
the Dutch East Indies, and elsewhere the communist parties did not succeed in playing major roles in these revolutions. To be sure, the Indian Congress Party contained a
left wing headed by Jawaharlal Nehru which found a
good deal of inspiration in communist ideas; and similar
intellectual currents were alive in other colonial countries.

But they did not yield benefit to the communist parties.
In China, the happy merger of the party with the revolutionary Kuo Min Tang was forcibly dissolved in 1926.
"Comrade" Chiang Kai-shek, officially still affiliated with
he Comintern, decimated the ranks of the Chinese Communist Party by a bloody purge and destroyed communist
hopes for years to come. The years of prosperity ended
with the Communist International better organized than
ever—strong parties and a widely ramified network of
auxiliary organizations, all of them in the hands of "safe"
leaders. Although the period had not brought any more
tangible political success, the spokesmen of international
communism were confident that new trouble was brewing for the capitalist world and that the years of prosperity were coming to an end. From the coming depression,
which they predicted accurately, the communist world expected the development of a new revolutionary situation
that would take global proportions.

The Great Depression predicted by the Comintern
came in 1929. It hit the capitalist world cruelly, ruined its
economy, created mass unemployment and misery. It
brought with it a general turn toward political radicalism,
which in Eastern Europe, Germany, and France destroyed democratic constitutionalism. It was a time of
profound crisis in the capitalist countries from which the
Communist International might have benefited, but did
not. The general shortcomings of the Third International
go far in explaining this. But some additional reasons
must be mentioned. First of all, the Great Depression coincided with the first and second five-year plans in the
Soviet Union, a time when Russia was busy with her own
problems and her leaders were unwilling to trouble themselves with international complications. Revolution making was as far as it could be from the minds of the men
in Moscow, who had plenty on their hands in trying to
industrialize their country and control their population.
The International in this period made a good deal of radical noise; but this was primarily to hide its actual policy
of isolationism.

The radical rhetoric was a function of the new policy line adopted by the International at this time, a policy of uncompromising leftism. It should by now have become clear that one of the major problems of communist policy making has always been to define the attitude of the party to other socialist parties. Just as the communist is ambivalent in his appraisal of the working class itself, at times being confident that the proletariat has become "conscious," at times despairing over its lack of consciousness, so his judgment changes about parties which, like his own, purport to speak for the workers. To be sure, the Comintern was founded with the specific purpose of making the gulf between communists and social-democrats unbridgeable. Lenin's own loathing of moderate socialism and its representatives was shared by his followers. And even when the International expressed the desire for an alliance between the two parties, the understanding was that the communists sought to support the socialists "as the noose supports the man who is being hanged." And yet, the actual policies of the Third International toward the moderate socialists were subject to considerable modifications. Whenever the Comintern was convinced that its very existence (or that of the USSR) was threatened by conservative or reactionary forces, it formed a defensive alliance with left-of-center liberals or moderate socialists, an alliance formed ostensibly to preserve constitutional democracy and the liberties associated with it. But its basic hostility toward the social democrats would break through in full force particularly in periods when a revolutionary situation was believed to be developing. At such times, a communist had to be on guard against the socialists, because in his opinion they were, after all, only the left wing of the bourgeoisie, and they could be expected to betray the revolution. When the time for great decisions draws near, it is always the unreliable ally who becomes the most dangerous enemy and must be unmasked and opposed.

And so, when the Western world was staggering under the blows of the economic crisis, when constitutional democracy was eroded by radicalism of the right and the left, the communist parties concentrated their fire on the socialist parties. As a result, the Comintern achieved partial success: "bourgeois democracy" in much of Continental Europe was destroyed. But the communist parties did not manage to take the second step which they had hoped and expected to take—to grab the power from the tottering capitalists. Instead, right-wing authoritarian regimes took over wherever constitutional democracy could not manage to maintain itself. These regimes came to power partly in the name of militant anticommunism; and once they were in power they usually proceeded to stamp out communism, together with the remnants of socialism and democratic liberalism. As a result, the most important communist parties outside the Soviet Union, together with some lesser ones, were destroyed almost completely. The vast political machinery of the Third International, built up with blood and tears and tremendous resources, was destroyed in one terrible blow.

Nor was the movement any more successful in the colonies and underdeveloped areas. In China, Comintern agents or Chinese leaders obedient to the commands of Moscow made futile attempts to stir up the urban masses. They were defeated by the lethargy of the workers, by the Kuo Min Tang, and by the Japanese invasion of Manchuria. Meanwhile, a little-known communist warlord, Mao Tse-tung, while paying lip service to Comintern instructions, silently began to build up the strength of the party on the basis of an overwhelmingly rural following— a proletarian party without a proletariat. In the northwestern part of China and also behind the lines of the Japanese (after they had occupied portions of China proper), substantial rural areas came under the authority of this communist party, so that, gradually and without attracting much notice in Comintern circles, the nucleus of a veritable communist republic developed.

A major reversal in policy was undertaken in 1935, not only as a result of the defeats we have just discussed, but more directly because of new international developments.

By this time it had become apparent that the Great Depression and the ensuing political crises would not lead to proletarian revolutions. Instead, they had produced fascist and authoritarian regimes which were not only militantly anticommunist but also militantly aggressive in international relations. The Soviet Union felt itself threatened by the clear and present danger of German and Japanese attacks. More than ever her leaders were concentrating their attention on the problems of economic and military growth and on instilling unquestioning loyalty and discipline into her population. But they also tried to secure themselves through action in the international arena.

From the beginning, the foreign policy of the USSR relied primarily, though not exclusively, on the device frequently used by powers that are weak and feel themselves threatened—this device is to seek allies among other weak, threatened, or dissatisfied powers, so as to confront the major powers with a protective alliance of the underdogs. The underdogs, or have-not powers with whom Soviet Russia cultivated mutually fruitful relations on this basis, included Germany, Italy, Japan, China, Iran, and Turkey. It should be noted that this policy was altogether unrelated to the real pursuits of the Communist International. If anything, these pursuits were in conflict with Soviet attempts to cement its alliances with the underdogs of the capitalist world of nations.

Now, in 1935, for the first time the policies of the International were geared immediately to the Soviet's policy of alliances. Alarmed by the military threat of German and Japanese power, Moscow's satellite parties adopted the policy of the Popular Front. Communist parties everywhere sought to ally themselves with, or even give unrewarded support to, any political group or government ready to resist fascism, national socialism, or other forms of government regarded as direct threats to the Soviet Union.

To be sure, attempts were made to use Popular Front arrangements or alliances for the purpose of weaning the masses away from moderate programs, to build up communist strength by taking command over socialist or liberal groups of one sort or another and thus to prepare for proletarian revolution. As a consequence, a good deal of ill feeling and distrust arose between the communist parties and the groups they sought to use or abuse. But, in general, the International and its affiliated parties tended to tone down their specifically communist aims and programs. The communist parties at least ostensibly transformed themselves into the left wing of liberal and moderate socialist parties. They came out as defenders of due process and constitutional government and, in international affairs, of collective security. The USSR entered the League of Nations, which for years it had denounced as the victors' club of the big imperialist states, and the Soviet spokesman, Maxim Litvinov, acquired the reputation of being the staunchest defender of global democracy. The Soviet government and its satellite parties went to great pains to persuade the world that the USSR itself was a thoroughly democratic country governed on the basis of a liberal constitution. In his interview with Roy Howard, in 1936, Stalin rejected the allegation that he or his government was interested in promoting world communism. How much of this line, if any, was deliberate deception is impossible to say. At least to some extent, the attempt to mobilize the forces of democracy against fascism and the like was made by Moscow with the expectation that it would fail (and would thereby reveal the hypocrisy of liberal democracy). Doubtless many communists preached liberal ideals only in order to show that under capitalism these ideals cannot be fulfilled. Perhaps Litvinov's disarmament proposals and communist attempts to safeguard civil liberties and constitutional democracy were similarly motivated. But the first impetus for these attempts undoubtedly came from the threats of aggression facing the USSR.[3]

In pursuit of the Popular Front policy, communist programs were not only toned down. Actually there were cases in which deliberate steps were taken to prevent or sabotage revolutions. In China, for instance, the Popular

Front policy compelled the communists to ally themselves with their archenemy, Chiang Kai-shek, against Japan and even to save his life and liberty after he had fallen into their hands through the kidnaping at Sian in 1936. The Chinese communists did so only with the greatest reluctance, many of them doubtless feeling that Moscow was betraying them. In Spain, the party faced a dilemma —either to support and promote the working-class revolution that had begun, and thereby endanger the war effort, or deliberately to postpone and stamp out the revolution for the purpose of winning the civil war. Without hesitation the party chose the latter course and lost both the war and the revolution.[4] In the United States, the Popular Front policy caused the party to support the New Deal, even though they had at first denounced it as a semifascist attempt to save capitalism from certain collapse.

It should also be remembered that the years of the Popular Front coincided with the Great Purge in the Soviet Union. The Western world was being challenged to defend constitutional democracy just at the time when police terror was celebrating bloody orgies in the USSR. This was, moreover, a period of national frenzy and intense xenophobia in Russia, and, whether by accident or design, foreign nationals were hit with especial ferocity by the purges. The Soviet Union, by this time, was the refuge of great numbers of foreign communists who had fled from political persecution in their own countries. These colonies of foreign communist leaders were decimated by the Great Purge, which virtually wiped out several communist parties. The work left unfinished by the Gestapo or similar institutions in Poland, Hungary, and other states was thus completed by the NKVD. Meanwhile, the entire purge orgy, with its open and secret trials, its fantastic confessions, had a chilling effect on many people in Western countries in sympathy with communism and so jeopardized the success of the Popular Front policy.[5]

In the end, the Popular Front policy turned out to be as much of a failure as all previous Comintern policies.

The communist parties did not succeed in making lasting alliances with any socialist parties, although numerous left-wing groups and associations in the Western democracies came under the influence of their new communist members (who had joined in obedience to Popular Front policy directives) and often voiced the party line. That line consisted in warnings against fascism, praises for liberal democracy, and assertions that the USSR in its domestic and foreign policies was the only country which consistently followed and promoted the ideals and precepts of liberal democracy, while in the Western democracies these ideals were being betrayed or in danger of being betrayed. Although some of these notions attained considerable popularity among intellectuals in England, France, the United States, and a few other countries between 1935 and 1938, the Communist International was unable to make these ideas pay off: the Western democracies did not yield to the prodding given them by Moscow and by their own left-of-center circles to resist German, Italian, or Japanese aggression. Instead, they followed the paths of "nonintervention" and "appeasement," which in the end led to the Munich pact of 1938. This pact marked the complete and utter failure of the Popular Front. Once again the Third International had miscalculated disastrously.[6]

From this point on, it was a moribund organization. In response to Munich, the USSR signed a treaty of friendship with the Third Reich in August of 1939, dismaying and rebuffing sympathizers and fellow travelers in the West and also many party members, who had supported the USSR and the party as the staunchest bastions against fascist aggression. As England and France girded their loins to fight at last against Nazi Germany, the Communist International advised its followers that the new war was an imperialist war—a family quarrel between imperialist nations and of no concern to the party of the proletariat. Instead, the workers were urged to sabotage the war effort, to resist emergency controls and the imposition of wartime hardships, and to desert from the armed forces. The small number of people who heeded this call attested to the lack of influence any of the communist parties had among the masses.[7]

The final reversal of Comintern policies was a natural consequence of Hitler's attack on the USSR in June of 1941. The Communist International automatically resumed the slogans of the Popular Front, this time with renewed vigor and with changes in emphasis. No longer was it necessary to goad the Western democracies into resistance to national socialism. Their will to resist was now assured; and, if it needed to be revived occasionally, this was accomplished far more advantageously by the Soviet government, now allied with the democracies, than by the communist parties. These parties had only one more function left—to persuade their followers that the only task for faithful communists now was to support the allied war effort. Workers in the West were to forget their grievances against capitalists. They were to do their best and make no demands. Racial, religious, or national minorities feeling the sting of discrimination were to shelve their complaints for the duration of the war and forget about their aims to gain equality. Rebellious nationalists in the colonies were to forget or postpone their demands for freedom and self-government and give their full support to the governments they had always been told to regard as their oppressors. Communist resistance groups in countries occupied by the enemy were urged to merge with, and even subject themselves to, noncommunist resistance forces, to give up their identity and goals so as not to jeopardize the war effort or embarrass the Soviet Union.[8]

It is obvious that instructions of this nature had not the slightest similarity to communist programs. Moreover, the USSR apparently regarded the very existence of the International as an embarrassment and a hindrance. In its efforts to cement the wartime alliance with the Western democracies, which Moscow considered essential for the successful defense of the Soviet Union, the Kremlin did not wish to remind its allies that it had once been the headquarters of the world revolution. That world revolution was not, for the time being, on the agenda. Consequently, without ceremony or fanfare, without even the pretense of going through elaborate formal procedures, the little side show or, as Stalin is reputed to have called the Communist International contemptuously, the "little shop" quietly closed its books and folded its tents. The year was 1943. It is ironic and perhaps significant that the international organization of communist parties was dissolved precisely at the time when for the first time since 1917 the international communist movement was about to achieve important gains. The battle of Stalingrad was the turning point of the war and of the history of the world in our century. The Soviet Union began to emerge as a major world power.[9]

8

The Soviet Union
Describes Itself

According to official Soviet rhetoric, the USSR no longer is a proletarian dictatorship but has turned into a socialist state of the toilers, in which exploitation and the class struggle have disappeared together with private property in the means of production. It is a state governed in accordance with a constitution which is more democratic than any other constitution past or present, because government is more truly representative of the people, and the rights of citizens are guaranteed more meaningfully than anywhere else.

After the completion of the second five-year plan, in the mid-thirties, the Soviet regime announced that the USSR had become a socialist society. It based this claim on the assertion that private enterprise had been eliminated completely with the abolition of the NEP and the collectivization of agriculture. Since now production proceeded according to a national plan presumably based on the needs of society rather than on the demands of the market—since, in other words, commodity production had been abolished—socialism was established by definition. This did not mean that the final goal of the communist movement had been reached. That final goal is communism, and party doctrine follows Lenin in making a careful distinction between socialism and communism. Communism is understood to incorporate the following features: an economy sufficiently productive to satisfy the material needs of all citizens and thus free them from material want; absolute equality of rewards, with the understanding that individuals will have different needs and different interests—equality of rewards then comes to mean the opportunity for every citizen freely to satisfy his own personal needs; universal rationality, or, as Soviet terminology expresses it, consciousness—a state in which all citizens have been raised to the level of consciousness hitherto attained only by the most advanced individuals, the vanguard; a universal collective conscience which persuades every citizen to work freely and cheerfully, and without expectation of reward, for the collective good—under communism, Lenin said, unrewarded work for the community will have become a habit. All these traits of communism imply that it is also without classes. All work will have become so mechanized that it will have turned into a routine everyone can perform. Or, perhaps, it will be so light a burden that people will be able to become skilled in many tasks. In any event, no longer will the division of labor divide men against men. In particular, all production will have become so mechanized or "automatized" that the differences between industry and agriculture, between city and country, will have been wiped out. Finally, under communism, institutions of domination will have become superfluous. Rule of men over men will have given way to the "administration of things" and to genuine collective self-government—the state will have withered away. Of all these features, voluntary work and equality of reward are singled out by Soviet doctrine as the principal ones; for communism is defined as a social order governed by the principle, "From each according to his ability; to each according to his need."

Socialism, in contrast, is the society which, once the capitalists have been expropriated, sets out to reach that final goal, communism, by means of economic growth and the education of the people for communism. By definition, therefore, this is a society in which abundance is not yet produced. But if there are wants or needs that remain unfilled, there is no equality of unfulfillment or misery. Since voluntary work for the common good has not yet become the habit of every healthy organism, incentives are still required to make people work. Incentives, however, imply a system of managed inequality, the exact amount of the rewards (in material goods, status, power, or other values) to be determined by the individual's performance or his value to the community. And so socialism is defined as that system which is functioning according to the principle, "From each according to his ability; to each according to his work."

The need for incentives (and, as we shall see, sanctions) gives this socialism some similarity with capitalist and precapitalist societies. While Soviet theory concedes this, it would stress the difference between the incentives in socialism and those operating in previous societies: socialist incentives, according to Soviet ideology, are more humane. Under feudalism, the main incentive was the knout—whoever did not perform to the satisfaction of the lord was whipped. Under capitalism, the main incentive was hunger—whoever did not compete successfully in the labor market starved to death. To be sure, the Soviet system also threatens its citizens with hunger if they do not pitch in; it has written this threat into its constitution, which contains the biblical words, "He who does not work, neither shall he eat," and makes them a guiding principle for Soviet society. At the same time, Soviet theory claims that the principal incentive under socialism is the expectation of greater reward, and, even more important, the desire for personal growth. Soviet citizens compete with each other not for the purpose of cutting each other's throats but in order to become more useful and more productive citizens. Soviet theory thus assumes a considerable amount of altruism, or, perhaps more correctly, of enlightened self-interest, because the expectation of reward is supported by the conviction that labor for the collectivity is labor for one's self. Since private property in the means of production has yielded to public ownership, the individual working for the government or the society is in fact working for himself, and the harder he works and the less reward he receives, the more quickly will he benefit from the general economic growth resulting from his and his fellow citizens' labor and deprivation. Thus, while rewarding those who produce above the general norm or who have scarce skills, the Soviet government expects its citizens in general to postpone gratification of their material needs for the sake of raising the common level of production.

Until the early 1930's, the Soviet regime tended to be apologetic about the resulting differences in reward and regard them as a temporary emergency measure. As a matter of fact, in the first years after the revolution, it had tried to foster equality as much as possible and especially to prevent party members and government officials from profiting materially from their positions of authority. While these measures to level society down to an equality of misery was never entirely successful, they worked within limits; and the rhetoric of equality prevailed for about fifteen years. Since then, Soviet theory has taken a more positive attitude toward differences in material reward and has denounced "equality mongering" as a petty-bourgeois deviation from, and a betrayal of, socialist ideas—as something hostile to Soviet socialism.

A very similar change in doctrine must be noted in a closely related problem—the differentiation in authority possessed by the citizens. Lenin's statement that after the revolution any female cook could take a turn at running the government was abandoned very quickly. But for a decade and a half after 1917 there was a cult of equality and a distrust of authority and rank, which may be explained in part by the fact that the individuals in positions of authority often were former tsarist officers or "bour-

geois specialists" such as engineers and managers. To
some extent, also, the cult of equality was a reaction
against the age-old Russian tradition of rank consciousness, which had pervaded military and civilian life. One of
the features of early Soviet administration, the custom of
managing public agencies by committees, was clearly a
result of this revulsion against authority as such. This
egalitarianism, too, was now abandoned and denounced.
It gave way to an authoritarian principle of individual
leadership (*edinonachalie*), after Stalin announced that in
Soviet society "cadres decide everything." The principle
of hierarchy in command and authority was thus made
part of the definition of socialism.[1]

Did the claim that socialism had been achieved imply
that Soviet Russia had become a classless society? By no
means. Classlessness is attributed only to the final stage,
communism. Then did this mean that a class struggle was
still raging in the socialist society? Again the answer is
no. To be sure, two different classes are acknowledged to
exist, classes that have different interests and different
relations to the means of production. One of these is the
working class (no longer called proletariat, because a
proletariat is defined as the class exploited by capitalism);
the other one is the peasantry. Out of both classes, who
are said to be held together by a firm and friendly alliance, rises an additional group, not a class, but only a
"layer." This is the intelligentsia, which in Soviet terminology denotes all who are not workers or peasants. That
means all white-collar and professional people, from
clerks and typists to movie stars, generals, and cabinet
ministers. The existence of these classes (plus one stratum) is thus acknowledged, and hence the existence of
different class interests and class consciousnesses. But a
conflict of classes is not admitted. Soviet theory asserts
that the interests of these classes do not conflict, that class
harmony and class collaboration characterize Soviet socialist society. For even though there are differences,
these differences are not as deep as class differences in
capitalism, because no class owns the means of produc-

tion. No class exploits another class. There is no leisure class; all Soviet citizens—workers, peasants, and intelligentsia—are "toilers."

There is yet another distinction Soviet theory makes among its citizens. That is a distinction between the toilers on the one hand and the most advanced members of the working class, who make up the membership of the Communist Party, on the other. The party is considered the most advanced organization of Soviet society because it knows the real interests of the workers, speaks for them, leads them, and represents them in word and in deed. The party is credited with outstanding accomplishments. It has led the Soviet people to emancipation from feudal and capitalist oppression and it now provides guidance and supervision to Soviet citizens in all their endeavors. The membership of the party comprises the most conscious and advanced persons in every type of Soviet organization and in every walk of life. Led by such outstanding geniuses as Lenin, Stalin, and Khrushchev, the party has always guided the Soviet people faultlessly, always accurately analyzing existing problems and situations, always correctly interpreting the interests of the people and finding the proper means toward the implementation of these interests. It has succeeded in this even though at times hostile elements have managed to worm themselves into the ranks of the party, even into very high places. Moreover, Marxism, which guides the party in its actions, is not easily mastered; and, while the party leadership has never wavered in the correct application of Marxist methods, even well-meaning members have at times deviated to the left or the right, succumbing either to the lure of antirevolutionary traitors or to the unproletarian influence of their own petty-bourgeois background. Whether or not such deviation is conscious, or willful, or based on evil intentions, objectively it makes the deviant member a counterrevolutionary. But the party has always saved its integrity by eliminating counterrevolutionaries. In recent years, it has been admitted further that in some matters even the party leadership went astray: under Stalin, it

fell victim to the "cult of personality" and allowed the
general secretary to arrogate excessive power to himself,
in violation of the principle of collective leadership. This
led to grave and dangerous mistakes; but, wherever possible, these mistakes have been corrected; and, wisened by
the experience, the party will not fall into this error again.
Soviet theory does not make it clear, however, what guarantees there are against the revival of the personality cult.

This, then, is the social structure of Soviet socialism, according to Soviet doctrine. It is a dynamic society, moving steadily toward all the transformations still required
to bring about communism. The party expects to achieve
this final goal within the foreseeable future. Several details
of the process by which it expects to achieve it are worthy
of our attention.

For one thing, Soviet doctrine asserts that the leap
from socialism to communism will be made without a revolution. It will indeed be a leap, but it will be made as a
result of gradual cumulative changes, and it will require
neither the violent overthrow of an existing social order
nor a system of domination. In Soviet socialist society, the
superstructure does not lag behind the development of
the forces of production, as it does in all other societies.
It does not therefore get in the way of economic progress.
On the contrary, it is a major agent of progress; and the
last of the great Russian revolutions was the work of the
Soviet government. This last revolution was the forcible
elimination of kulaks and NEP men—the abolition of private enterprise; and it was a "revolution from above."
Still, while the bolshevik revolution, according to Soviet
theory, aligned the superstructure with the base, it still is a
superstructure; and, as we know, this must disappear under full-fledged communism. Left-wing critics of the
Stalin regime in the early 1920's postulated a "third revolution" which would have to remove the superstructure.
Soviet theory, however, asserts that the superstructure will
simply wither away after it has done its job fully.

Marxism in its original form incorporated a theory of
lag; the relations of production and the superstructure of

traditions, mores, institutions, and ideologies growing out of these relations lagged behind the development of productive forces and became an obstacle to further progress. In Soviet doctrine, this relationship has been reversed. Soviet theory concedes that there is some lag; for instance, the continued maintenance of some private property in farming and of cooperative private enterprise in various crafts is regarded as a hang-over from the capitalist past which sooner or later must be removed in order to align the relations of production with the productive forces. But, in the main, consciousness as well as social relations, in Soviet socialism, are regarded as being ahead of the development of the forces of production and as instruments to help build them up. The party's main tool in this is the *state,* which therefore acquires positive value as a force of progress. Formerly, the state was seen as a product of class struggle. Now there is no class struggle, according to Soviet theory, even though a conflict of interests is still acknowledged, such as the conflict between the individual's "immediate" and his "real" interests. Some communists argued that therefore there was no justification for the state. But the party rejects this argument. We shall discuss the main grounds for this rejection below. Here we note only that the party justifies the state as an essential instrument for planning, organizing, and managing some of the transformations necessary to bring about the transition to communism, especially the growth of the forces of production. The state is the entrepreneur of socialism. By promoting production, it creates the preconditions for its own withering away. Soviet theory indignantly rejects the idea that the Soviet state might have become, or might in the future become, the instrument of rule for a privileged elite. Instead, it asserts (without being about to prove this except by tautological definitions) that the contradictions of Soviet society, including the clash between rich and poor, powerful and subordinate, will never entrench themselves and that the privileged elite expresses the common interest. While the capitalist state is the product of class antagonisms which

it then helps to perpetuate, the Soviet state will resolve
class antagonisms by increasing production.*

Additional agents of change and progress, according to
Soviet doctrine, are *criticism and self-criticism,* as well as
socialist morality—in short, the individual's intellectual
awareness of his own and his fellow citizens' shortcomings, the free discussion of these failings in communal meetings and in media of mass communication, and
the moral determination to overcome them and contribute to the best of one's ability, to be loyal and patriotic
and confident of ultimate success. Failures in the Soviet
system, poor performance of individuals or organizations,
even criminality, neurosis, and insanity, according to
Soviet theory, can usually be explained by the inadequate
consciousness or insufficient morality of some members of
society. What else could be their cause, since the system
itself is beyond criticism? Moreover, Soviet psychology
assumes that all people are basically equal—not to believe
this would be to succumb to myths about race and in-
heritance. But if all human beings are equally endowed
with intellectual and physical potentialities, differences in
performance can be explained only by differences in will
and application.

One of the cornerstones of Soviet doctrine is the concept of *socialism in a single country.* We remember that
the bolsheviks seized power in the firm expectation that
the Russian revolution would lead to proletarian revolutions in the entire civilized world. We have indicated

* Against this, a growing number of analysts assert that
Soviet society, like all modern industrial societies, is bound to
develop into a stratified class society in which the industrial
managers will sooner or later obtain control because they control
the essential means of production. Developed as early as 1918
by the Polish socialist Waclaw Machajski, this theme was later
picked up by James Burnham, *The Managerial Revolution* (New
York, 1941), and repeated, with slight modifications, by
Georg Achminov, *Die Macht im Hintergrund* (Ulm, 1950)
and Milovan Djilas, *The New Class* (New York, 1957). The
thesis is related to the pessimistic theories of both Roberto
Michels and Leon Trotsky about inevitable bureaucratic per-
versions of socialism.

why they expected this and why without world revolution
their own success made little or no sense to them. In signing the Treaty of Brest Litovsk, the Soviet regime chose
coexistence with capitalism; but it did so only in the belief
that the world revolution was still developing and needed
only a chance to "catch its breath." After the abortive
German revolutions of 1921 and 1923 it became clear to
many Soviet leaders that the world revolution was going
to take its time. The Communist International in its 1924
congress decided that world capitalism had entered a
period of stabilization and that the world as a whole was
in a transitional period between the Russian revolution
and the world revolution, a period during which the Soviet
regime would have to coexist with the capitalist countries
and find a *modus vivendi* with them.* Some members of
the party pointed out that in this case the revolution would
have been in vain, a senseless and costly adventure likely
to discredit the Marxist movement as a whole. The Trotsky faction countered the doctrine of the stabilization
of capitalism first by denying it and then by calling for
vigorous revolutionary action on a global scale. They
argued that the stabilization of capitalism was a passing
phenomenon and that excessive attention paid to it
amounted to opportunism and a betrayal of the revolution.
Instead of adjusting to the ephemeral prosperity and sta-
bility of the capitalist world, the party should prepare for
the new revolutionary upheavals that would inevitably ac-
company the equally inevitable end of stabilization. Not
only that, the party ought to do its share to undermine
capitalism and thus to promote and speed up the development of a new revolutionary situation. Here we have the
global aspect of Trotsky's theory of "permanent revolution."

Against the arguments of the Trotsky faction the Stalin–

* Coexistence does not necessarily mean *peaceful* coexistence; Lenin's theories also contain the idea of an inevitable
clash between the "camps" of capitalism and socialism, and
he described the entire transition period between capitalism
and socialism as an era of world wars and revolutions.

Bukharin faction developed its theory of socialism in one country. They conceded that the revolution could never be completed, nor any of its achievements be safe, before the entire world (or a large portion of it) had become communist. But even though the achievements of the revolution would not be safe as long as they remained isolated in one country, this was no reason for despair. Even under such limiting conditions, socialism could be built in a single country, even a backward country like Russia. And to deny this possibility, they said, was defeatism and menshevik pusillanimity. To be cowed by economic conditions or to emphasize the immaturity of any society for socialism, they argued, was shallow determinism. For a bolshevik, social and economic conditions are not insurmountable obstacles but a spur to action. There is nothing that resolute action by the party cannot overcome.

With the victory of Stalin, the doctrine of socialism in a single country became party dogma, and with it the idea that a long transition period comes between the Russian Revolution and the completion of the world revolution. Two main implications were inherent in this: the recognition of *coexistence* as an inescapable necessity for the duration of the transition period, and the admission that socialism confined to one country (and a backward one at that) would look different from what the revolutionaries of 1917 had imagined and hoped it would look. These two implications are closely related to each other, the former being responsible for the latter. For it is a central point in Soviet theory to blame the exigencies of coexistence (termed "capitalist encirclement") for any disappointing features of Soviet socialism. In particular, capitalist encirclement is cited as the main reason why the state has not yet withered away, as a Marxist ought to have expected once he was told that exploitation and the class struggle had been abolished. Indeed, once the party had announced that socialism had been reached, there seem to have been queries by party members whether the state could now be expected to wither away. In answering with a decided "no," the party stressed capitalist encirclement, but also alleged that coexistence had its domestic equivalents too, in that some elements of Soviet society were still susceptible to insidious capitalist influence from outside. A strong state, including a mighty army and a police force, was thus required to keep capitalism at bay, and the stronger it was made, the more quickly and surely would it wither away.* While Soviet theory thus makes coexistence responsible for repressive features of Soviet society, Marxists who are antagonistic to the USSR have argued that the repressive nature of Soviet society is responsible for coexistence. The revolution occurred first in a backward country not mature for socialism. Whether this is to be blamed on bolshevik adventurism or whether it was unavoidable is controversial. In any event, in a backward country only a sad caricature of socialism could be developed. This it is argued, has so discredited revolutionary Marxism as a whole that it has perverted the normal course of history and enabled capitalism to entrench itself in the Western world, where true socialism might otherwise have been created after a proletarian revolution.

Soviet theory does not acknowledge the need to be apologetic about anything. True, the state has not yet withered away. But it is, after all, a most acceptable state, a constitutional democracy of a superior type, in which democracy is not just a phrase but a reality. Government by soviets, it is claimed, is the most ideal form of representative democracy because it gives the common man a better chance for direct control of, or participation in, the process of government than any other institution. Being a sensitive barometer of public opinion, Soviet government institutions allegedly do not require checks and balances

* Herbert Marcuse in *Soviet Marxism* (New York, 1958), pp. 51-55, rightly points out that this is a theory of containment: according to Soviet theory imperialism seeks to destroy the world revolution. He has shown that, despite modifications and reservations in their theory, the actual strategy of world communism has always presupposed that the revolution in the West had little chance, and that communist action should always be on the defensive.

or a division of powers. Soviet government is good government; and good government ought not to be curbed by such devices.

The Soviet constitution, it is claimed further, fulfills liberal ideals by being a federal constitution. The Union of Socialist Soviet Republics is a voluntary federation of free nations, each one of which is at liberty to determine its own national destiny, even to the point of seceding from the USSR. That in fact this destiny consists in merging with the other nations making up the Soviet Union is taken for granted by Soviet theory; and anyone actually advocating secession from the Union would at once be recognized as an enemy of proletarian internationalism, and dealt with accordingly. The liberties granted by the most democratic of all constitutions are meaningful only as long as they are not abused by the class enemy.

In addition to providing self-determination for all nations of Soviet society, the constitution of 1936, more amply than any other constitution, provides the individual citizens with basic rights. It grants not only the customary freedoms of speech, assembly, the press, and religious belief; it also outlaws discrimination based on sex, race, religion, or national origin. And, finally, it grants all citizens the right to employment, to an education, and to medical and other assistance in case of need. It thus complements political rights with social and economic rights.

Soviet theoreticians point out that, unlike all previous constitutions, the Soviet constitution also provides guarantees for these rights and thus makes them meaningful. What good is the capitalist freedom of the press to the workers who do not have the money to start a newspaper or run a television station? How valid is the freedom of assembly in societies where club houses or meeting halls are for hire or purchase only to those who are able to pay? In the USSR these and other rights and liberties are guaranteed by the fact that assembly halls and media of mass communication, as well as all the means of production, have been taken away from the capitalists and are now in the hands of the party and other organizations representing the will of the people, just as Soviet democracy is made truly representative by the fact that its informal processes, such as the nominations and selection of candidates for public office, are largely in the hands of the party, the trade unions, and other organizations expressing the interests of the toilers.

According to Soviet doctrine, the USSR is not only the most democratic state in the world, it is also the chief defender of democracy in international affairs. Lacking aggressive tendencies, the Soviet Union since its inception has consistently played a progressive role in world politics. Therefore it is supported loyally not only by almost all its own citizens but also by all truly class-conscious workers in the whole world.

In recent years, Soviet ideology has turned its attention to the problem of the transition from socialism to communism. We have noted that this was to take the form of a gradual, nonviolent transition. In his last essay, published shortly before the Nineteenth Congress of the party, Josef Stalin spelled out some of the preconditions for this transition. Communism would come within sight once the Soviet economy was able to raise real wages for the entire population to a specified level—and by extrapolating the rate of growth from records of Soviet productivity, economists could estimate that communism was still a few decades away. Further, Stalin postulated a major transformation of the collective farms before communism could be placed on the agenda, and a number of other conditions. On the basis of Stalin's calculations, the prospect of attaining communism in the near future receded. In retrospect, Stalin's conclusion can be interpreted as manifesting a conservative attitude. Stalin obviously meant to imply that any deviation from his own methods of government would be premature; the time was not yet ripe for any major changes. His successor, however, has become more optimistic. Nikita Khrushchev has announced several times that Soviet society is now entering the stage of gradual transition from socialism to communism. In particular, he has asserted that the state has already begun to wither away, and to support this assertion he refers to various measures taken by his regime to decentralize administration, place some functions of government in the hands of neighborhood groups and other grass-roots agencies, and curb the powers of the political police.

Soviet ideologists have spent considerable effort on the elaboration of this thesis. In their writings, they stress the idea that in the future, life will be more communal and less individualistic than heretofore. Ongoing pilot projects heralding thoroughgoing reforms in administration, education, economic management, and other endeavors show that these writings, far from being speculative, are in fact blueprints of an impending transformation of the Soviet way of life. A milestone in this process of planning for communism was the adoption of a new party platform by the Twenty-second Congress of the Communist Party, in the fall of 1961.[2]

Here and there, in passing, we have noted differences between the Soviet theory of state and the spirit of Marxist thought. We have even ventured to state that Soviet theory is in decided opposition to the humanist ethics and the radical criticism inherent in Marxism. Soviet theoreticians would not, of course, agree with this. They would, rather, assert that the history of the Russian Revolution, the development of Soviet society, and the doctrines of Soviet ideology are all in full correspondence with Marxist ideas. To make Marxism fit Soviet history and ideology, it has been transformed, in the USSR, into a dogmatic philosophy bearing some striking similarities both to Thomist philosophy and to the scientific clichés of the Victorian age. Its more abstract branch, corresponding to what Western philosophers would call ontology, epistemology, logic, and the philosophy of science or nature, is called "dialectical materialism." The parts dealing with anthropology and psychology, ethics, aesthetics, and the philosophy of history are called "historical materialism."

In both branches, a catechism of philosophic laws has been abstracted from the writings of Marx, Engels, Lenin, and Stalin, laws which are said to describe the nature of all phenomena, social as well as nonsocial, in the universe. This philosophy affirms the objective reality of all phenomena and characterizes this reality as capable of being known by man. It defines the substance of all reality as matter and ascribes to all material phenomena certain dynamic qualities, such as contradictoriness and motion, or change. Dialectical materialism further spells out the patterns of interrelationships between material phenomena, such as the multiple chain of causality relating all phenomena to each other, but especially the laws of motion of matter, or, as we might say, the morphology of change. As for historical materialism, it is a catechism of the most general assumptions and methods used by Marx, Engels, Lenin, and Stalin in describing and analyzing social phenomena.

Marx, and even more Engels, manifested positivistic tendencies amounting to a rejection of philosophy. Soviet philosophy opposes this positivistic attitude. It does not follow Engels in identifying philosophy with the method of natural and social science, nor restrict it to logic and the history of ideas. Instead, it recognizes philosophy as a branch of learning distinct from natural and social science, even though the boundaries between philosophy and science have never been defined satisfactorily. The result of this dualism is that scientific pursuits are, as it were, made subservient to, or brought into line with, philosophic dogma, in a fashion comparable to the manner in which the Church subordinates the rational pursuit of knowledge to the acceptance of revealed truth. In both cases, scientific findings are recognized as valid only as long as they do not conflict with the established dogma. In both cases, also, it is taken for granted that the independent, rational search for scientific truth cannot possibly come into conflict with the dogma.

Soviet theory expresses this relationship in somewhat oblique fashion by asserting that all science is, and must

be, partisan, or in line with the spirit of the party. This
conformance to the party's policies and beliefs is called
partiinost'. Its imposition on everyone engaged in intellectual pursuits is justified by the party in the following
manner. All knowledge, they argue, is the reflection or
expression of some class interest. In all fields of knowledge, therefore, there are feudal, bourgeois, petty-bourgeois, and proletarian schools. There cannot be any neu-
trality. Even those who believe they are neutral or who
think that their fields of endeavor are far removed from
politics will in fact ("objectively") reflect the point of
view of one or another class. Now, Marx has shown, according to Soviet arguments, that the class consciousness
of the proletariat is true consciousness, whereas the consciousness of all other classes is false, ideological. Only in
the consciousness of the proletariat does class interest lead
to the emergence of truth unvarnished and undistorted. It
follows from this that in every field of knowledge the
search for truth will be successful only as long as
the scholar wholeheartedly adopts the point of view of the
working class. And since this point of view is expressed
best by the Communist Party, no scientific truth can stand
which conflicts in any way with the party's views, the
party line. Science, social as well as natural, including the
purest research in physics, biology, or mathematics, must
be pervaded with the spirit of *partiinost'*. In effect, this
means that in any realm of knowledge where the party
has expressed a definite opinion, it has been, until very
recently, virtually impossible to engage in discussion with
Soviet scholars, because, imbued with *partiinost'*, they
could not deviate from the accepted line or even the accepted terminology and were obliged to label any disagreement with their views or their vocabulary as the
ideology of the class enemy. Thus scientific truth could
not (and perhaps still today cannot) be pursued freely,
and truths conflicting with the party line are declared
falsehoods. As a result, more than one branch of Soviet
science has suffered lasting damage. But what we have
said applies with particular force in the social sciences,

where the party line has been refined and defined with so much precision that it seems to consist of inflexible magic formulas—a catechism or a litany which, according to Marcuse, does in fact function as magic; or, to say the least, social science is used for the purposes of public relations, and the principles of advertising are in eternal conflict with the search for truth. Where the inflexible formulas developed in social science are changed ever so slightly, we must always suspect changes in party policy or party views. Soviet ideology thus serves as an esoteric code of communications easily read by the initiated but decipherable also by the informed outsider.[3]

The transformation of theory into catechism is not, however, restricted to the social sciences but applies also in the more "remote" areas of knowledge and ideology. The reason for this is simple. If we are right in asserting that Soviet social theory serves mainly to obscure and veil the clash between the idea and the reality of socialism, if its dogmas are to pervert the ideals of liberty, equality, and brotherhood by affirming that socialism has been attained, then the ideals thus perverted or betrayed will tend to retreat into the "inner emigration" of seemingly remote and neutral areas—art, philosophy, and science. But here too they are dangerous to the regime, and the party has tried very hard to ferret them out. There is therefore no safe place for an inner emigration in the Soviet Union, at least not in the intellectual realm.

Lest this picture be considered one-sided and overdrawn, we should, perhaps, add two qualifications. First, despite the tendencies just described, there have been some branches of social science in which respectable scholarly work has always been done. Even when speaking of the Stalin period, therefore, we should not underestimate the ability of Soviet social scientists to engage in significant research. But a second point which concerns the erosion of dogma, or at least of dogmatic rigidity, in Soviet intellectual life is more important. We have already mentioned this loosening up, but we should add now that in recent months, the pace of this process seems to have speeded up considerably. If a few years ago we could say that the higher ranks of the party were allowed freedom of discussion (though not yet freedom of speech), it now appears that it is practiced far more widely and far more openly than Western scholars would have believed possible, even in recent years. In line with this, Soviet social science, too, may emerge from its subsidiary role as a mere exercise in public relations.

9

The Soviet Way of Life

A political scientist not committed to the Soviet ideology would doubtless, in describing the Soviet way of life, include some generalizations about the power structure (who actually commands or makes decisions, and what gives them the authority?); about decision-making procedures—the government apparatus, the legislative process, the structure of public administration; about strains in this machinery and the informal safety valves or corrective processes that make it continue to function; about sanctions and rewards offered to the population; about classes and social mobility; and about the degree of autonomy granted to individuals and groups. He might also investigate to what extent these social relationships correspond with different value systems, his own or that of his own community and also that of Soviet ideology. In presenting my own attempt at a description of Soviet society, I must apologize for the temerity of trying to condense such a complex and controversial theme into one brief chapter. Since this can be done only by omitting all detail and by overgeneralizing, the result can obviously be no more than an interpretive essay, in which every sentence is subject to challenge.*

To set the scene, we must describe the Soviet Union as an underdeveloped country engaged in a crash program to exploit its resources and outstrip the Western world in productivity and economic potential. It comprises a population of many languages, races, religions, and cultures, which, one generation ago, consisted primarily of rural people, peasants or nomads, on a level of technology, literacy, and productivity below that of urban and industrial Europe and North America. These were people without a strong tradition of self-government, yet they were rebellious against their ruling elites. About thirty years ago the Communist Party ruling over these people decided to make an all-out effort to industrialize their country as rapidly as possible. Whether this was a decision which sooner or later had to be taken, regardless of who was in power or what motives guided him, is a highly controversial question and must be left unanswered here. In any event, the decision was taken.

To carry it out, the Soviet social system had to undergo a number of adjustments, and the party had to take certain broad measures. Industrialization of an undeveloped economy requires, first of all, the marshaling of all material and human resources, hence an austerity regime in which every available scrap of energy is expended for the construction effort and every ounce of material resource that can be diverted from consumption is invested. Rapid industrialization, in other words, calls for continued low living standards and forbids consumer sovereignty. This applies all the more to a revolutionary regime surrounded by hostile neighbors, who cannot be expected to help the industrialization effort by large-scale material and technical assistance or long-term credits. The Soviet Union was forced to pull itself out of the morass of backwardness by its own bootstraps. From all this it becomes clear that, secondly, industrialization under such circumstances can be accomplished only through

* For one of the most recent attempts to describe the Soviet social system, see the discussion by Brzezinski, Meyer, and Tucker on "The Nature of the Soviet System," in *Slavic Review*, vol. XX, No. 3 (October 1961), pp. 351-388.

central organization and strict discipline, including a managed system of rewards and sanctions. While centralized planning and organized inequality are not necessarily incompatible with political liberty and representative democracy, it is nonetheless obvious that the planners and managers themselves are likely to look at constitutional democracy as a luxury which a backward country in the process of rapid industrialization cannot afford. And, if we look at the ruthlessness of the Soviet regime and at the starkness of the material austerity it imposed on its population, we have to conclude that such measures could have been carried out only by a powerful dictatorship ruling against the will of the people.

Forced saving and political dictatorship alone, however, are not sufficient. One more measure is required to achieve industrialization in a backward country; that is the training of the population for life in the machine age. Americans ought to be familiar with the adjustments this transformation in the way of life requires, with the difficulty of shedding traditions, beliefs, and behavior patterns that have become dysfunctional in the machine age. We all know the helplessness of the country hick stranded in the big city, the small-town folks' stubborn resistance against, and resentment of, the ways of the metropolis. We know the pains of adjustment in the style of life that are being suffered as America transforms herself from a country of farmers and petty merchants into a modern industrial and corporate giant. These pains of acculturation are intensified many times when a country like Russia engages in a crash program of industrialization. They are intensified because Soviet Russia has attempted to do in one generation what America has been doing for the last 150 years, and because the cultural level from which most of Russia started was even more remote from the way of life of the atomic age than was the society of Jefferson or Jackson. Lenin, for one, was aware of the magnitude and rapidity of the transformation he wished to bring about and fittingly called it a cultural revolution. In my opinion, this cultural revolution is the most difficult of all the tasks which the Russian Communist Party has set itself.

Power Structure

In describing the social relationships that have grown out of these problems, let us begin by a summary of the power structure in Soviet society. In his book on the process of politics in the United States, David Truman distinguishes between two major types of government existing in the modern world, constitutional government and corporate government. In describing the latter, he is concerned primarily with the manner in which such associations as business corporations and organized interest groups manage their affairs. But I believe we can easily apply his model to the Soviet Union as a whole. Some of its key features include the differentiation between the functions of the owner and the manager; the hierarchic command system of decision-making, which must be contrasted to responsible and representative government; the bureaucratic (rather than democratic) division of powers; and the servile and subject status of the lower ranks, for whom final recourse against the commands of the organization lies only outside that organization. One of the principal differences between a Western corporation and the USSR therefore lies in the fact that the aggrieved employee of a Western corporation can quit the organization more readily than a Soviet citizen, who in most cases has no possibility whatsoever of escaping from his society; and, short of quitting, the employee can appeal to authorities outside his corporation. Despite this and other major differences, I think it is useful to compare the USSR to a giant corporate enterprise, in order to understand some of its structural features.

It is difficult to define the owners of USSR, Incorporated, just as it is difficult to define precisely who owns General Motors. Certainly some own it more than others; or we might say that the quality of ownership varies with the quantity. Ownership of a few shares entitles one to a small share of the profits, while ownership of a substantial portfolio carries with it the right to sit on the Board of Directors, which hires and fires the managers and sets policies for the corporation. If we are right in saying that, for practical purposes, the Communist Party might be said to own the Soviet Union, we have to understand that the ownership functions of the rank and file party member are no more meaningful than those of Aunt Lucy, who owns a share of AT&T. Let me add at once that the Communist Party does not have legal title to the USSR and does not claim it. Ownership, however, may be defined not only in legal but also in sociological terms. In the latter case, ownership is established as soon as individuals or groups behave *as if they owned* an enterprise. And the Communist Party of the Soviet Union, especially its "Board of Directors," certainly does so behave. It treats the country as if it were its property. To use a traditional term of political science, the party acts as the *sovereign* in the Soviet Union—and, historically as well as philosophically, the concepts of sovereignty and property are virtually synonymous. To be sure, just as in the Western corporation ownership and management functions are tending more and more to be united in the same persons, so in the enterprise USSR, Incorporated, party members and managers (such as government officials) are often the same persons. And yet, a significant number of party members function solely as party administrators. They are the inner core of the party, the *aktiv*, as it is called in the Soviet Union, whose most successful members form the majority of such policy-making directorates as the Central Committee, the Secretariat, and the Presidium. If we speak of the party as the sovereign owner of the USSR, then, it seems, we must mean particularly the party *aktiv*, a ruling elite about whose size, composition, and informal structure we have only the sketchiest information. It, too, is meant by the Soviet citizen when he talks about "the party."

The party itself is much larger than its active core, for it includes the millions of members who are active pro-

fessionally in other pursuits, and whose party membership is therefore in the nature of additional duty. The size
and character of this membership has fluctuated. Today it
comprises roughly ten million, or 4 per cent of the population (or roughly 8 per cent of the population of voting
age). It is today a *cadre party,* which means that its members are selected from those citizens who occupy positions
of respect, responsibility, and authority in all the many
professions or pursuits to which Soviet citizens may be
devoted. One might be tempted to say that the party re-
cruits those members of Soviet society who in our society
would become members of country clubs, although the
criterion for selection is not wealth but managerial or
technical responsibility. Like membership in a country club,
party membership is at times an indispensable help in
furthering an individual's career or even a precondition
for various sensitive or responsible assignments. Unlike
country-club membership, however, it does not promote
the pursuit of golf, swimming, dancing, or other diver-
sions. Instead, it tends to become an arduous and onerous
additional duty. Party members are expected to be active
in the various party activities; they are supposed to educate
themselves further in the history and ideology of the party;
and, finally, they are assumed to lead exemplary lives as
model citizens. To have been selected by the party and
afterward found unworthy carries a stigma comparable to
that of the unfrocked priest.[1]

As the sovereign owner of Soviet society, the party (in
its highest organizations) not only makes the basic decisions of public policy; on all its levels of organization it
also sees to it that these decisions are carried out. It concerns itself, furthermore, with the selection and assign-
ment of the top managers in all fields of endeavor and,
finally, strives to propagate its views among the population. We might compare the individual party member to
the information and education officer in our armed forces,
who is supposed to inform the men about current world
affairs to tell them "what they are fighting for" or "whom
they are fighting against." In addition, the party acts as

the cheerleader of Soviet society, who through rallies, demonstrations, and publicity of various kinds seeks to build enthusiasm and morale. In everything that is done in Soviet society, the party claims to represent the people, to act in their name and in their behalf and for their bene-fit. Such claims cannot, of course, be proven and will be self-evident only to those who are already convinced. Among the population of the Soviet Union, there doubt-less are people so convinced, and also people who are not. The evidence suggests that various members of Soviet society admire the party, or tolerate it as a necessary evil, or hate it with all their heart. The gulf between the party and the people seems to be deepest in rural areas and among the national minorities. In the countryside, the Communist Party at times appears like an army of occu-pation or a militant church *in partibus infidelium,* while in Central Asia, Buriat-Mongolia, and other minority areas it assumes some of the aspects of a colonial adminis-tration (although there are significant differences between the "colonialism" of the Soviet Union and that of Western nations).

The organization of the party is well adapted to its various tasks. Apart from the strong predominance of centralistic tendencies and the absence of any meaningful democratic procedures, the most notable feature is the mixture of territorial with functional principles of organ-ization. On the higher levels, the party is subdivided into regional, provincial, local, and similar territorial organiza-tions, all of which, together with the all-Union headquar-ters in Moscow, have usually had staff organizations dealing with the functional divisions of Soviet life and activities—the economy, the armed forces, educaton, art, youth activities, national minorities, and the like. At the grass-roots level, however, the territorial principle is aban-doned for the functional one: with few exceptions, the party primary organizations (which have evolved from the conspiratorial cells of prerevolutionary days) are formed within economic or administrative organizations, such as workshops, farms, scientific institutes, army units, or government offices. The party unit thus formed takes charge, as it were, of the organization, regards it as "its own," and functions as a representative of the sovereign. The party primary organization is composed only of members of the parent body—a committee of it, in a sense; and it does act as some sort of steering committee. But, even though formed only of men and women who work in the organization, it is in reality the *direct* representative of the entire party.

I deliberately stress the word *direct*. For, after all, the ministry, or the regional planning and executive organization (Sovnarkhoz) which recently has been created, and also the bank, the public attorney, and other supervisory or command organizations including the political police —all represent the party, however indirectly. All nonparty organizations in the USSR are, in effect, departments or divisions of the over-all enterprise, USSR, Incorporated.

Any Soviet organization, economic, administrative, cultural, military, or what not, is subjected to the party through numerous command or supervisory channels at one and the same time; and Soviet society can therefore be seen as an administrative maze of parallel hierarchies. We may speak of the trinity of party, government, and police as the main pillars of this structure; or, looking at the economic enterprise, we may see that trinity dissolve into a multiplicity of legal, financial, economic, political, and police hierarchies, which may be working in harmony or may be vying with each other for control or jurisdiction. Whether separately or jointly, however, they all impose their particular tasks on the managers and lower personnel of the given unit.

Chief among the party's agencies in managing the country is the government, which includes not only most of the legislative, administrative, judicial, military, and penal institutions that are part of all modern governments, but also the entire economy, all educational and scientific pursuits, health services, and even entertainment and cultural endeavors. Certain processes of this government can be studied more easily than others and are therefore better known. Not known at all among Western students of the Soviet way of life is the legislative process. The constitution notwithstanding, policy decisions taking the form of laws, regulations, or decrees are discussed, formulated, and adopted behind closed doors, and we have only the scantiest information even concerning who discusses them, what the procedures are, and so forth. It is clear, however, that the major task which the enterprise USSR, Incorporated, has set itself is the task of production, or better, of rapid economic growth. In Soviet rhetoric, the task is defined as one of catching up with, and outstripping, the USA in production and productivity.[2]

The major political decisions for the managers of the enterprise during any one period are therefore the production plan and its supplementary decisions. Supplementary directives include financial plans, raw materials, utilization plans, labor plans, and others. The shaping of all these and the major production plans is a complex and continual operation based on information regarding available resources and skills, on experience regarding past performance, and on the political decision regarding priorities in production. The execution of the plan is the responsibility of the Council of Ministers, which used to include production ministries, just as a corporation includes production divisions, but which has recently delegated a great amount of work in administering and even shaping production plans to regional planning organizations. Through various channels, the commands of the Council of Ministers are conveyed to the principal economic units, the factories or enterprises, and, in modified fashion, the state farms and collective farms.

In accordance with the principle of individual managerial responsibility, the Soviet enterprise is given a certain degree of autonomy, even to the point of making it a juridical person. It is set up to resemble a business firm, with its own capital and cash resources. It deals with other enterprises of the Soviet economy through the means of contracts; and where there are contracts, there is a system

of laws governing contractual relationships, and a court
system to enforce them. Unlike a Western firm, however,
the Soviet enterprise in its various activities of buying,
selling, hiring, pricing, and production planning is subjected to the plan and to the controls of its numerous
superior agencies. And yet, restricted as his discretion is,
the director of a Soviet firm is responsible not only for ad-
herence to the various plans, laws, and directives specify-
ing permissible ranges of the use of materials, labor,
credit, and the like; his firm is also supposed to operate
at a profit; and, most of all, it is to meet or outstrip the
production goals handed down from the planning authorities. Under such multiple pressures, with high rewards
offered for outstanding performance and severe sanctions imposed for a poor showing, the Soviet production
manager has become part of a rat race very similar to
that in which his American colleague is engaged. Similar
conditions, moreover, are imposed on responsible personnel in noneconomic fields—physicians, artists, teachers, scholars, administrators, and even members of the
working class itself. The rat race is as all-pervasive in
Soviet society as it is in America.

In the Soviet Union, it is caused by a coincidence of
various factors. For one thing, the party asks all citizens,
high and low, to work their very hardest and give their
very best. The rule of this performance principle, as Marcuse calls it, is enforced not only by pitting fellow citizens
and rival organizations against each other in managed
competition but also by manipulating rewards in such a
fashion that only peak performance is rewarded ade-
quately. Secondly, the rat race is a function of the multiplicity of authorities imposing often conflicting standards
of behavior on the administrator. Whatever a Soviet
manager does, he is often forced to violate some standards
in order to satisfy others, because taken together all the
commands he has been given are impossible to carry out.
While at first glance the result of this is inefficiency and
chaos, it may nonetheless be a very satisfactory and efficient method of management for the party. Through its

many agencies, it enforces its standards selectively and therefore wields a complex administrative machinery that is very sensitive to subtle changes in policy. Such changes need not be announced formally but can be signaled by a slight shift in the selective enforcement of multiple standards. The party enjoys not only the possibility of manipulating the society but also the privilege of not having to contradict itself, while the lower managerial personnel take all the risks. They are struck with sanctions when shifts occur.[3]

Finally, the rat race in the Soviet Union is aggravated by the personal insecurity of the superiors, who are compelled to engage in struggles for jurisdiction, control, and authority. The subordinate administrator therefore must not only follow all directives given him but also beware of excessively close connections with a superior official who is going to be a loser. Much is written in the Western world about the ramifications of this kind of power struggle in the Soviet elite. But we know next to nothing concrete about it. All we can say with some degree of certainty is that the development of Soviet Russia into a modern industrial society has brought with it tendencies of unmeasurable strength toward the differentiation of special groups within the power elite, tendencies similar to those characterizing Western societies. Such groups, to which we can attribute different and conflicting interests, are based on loyalty to leaders, commitment to diverging policies, fields of professional specialization, or identification with particular regions or localities. In the concrete, these various interests doubtless overlap and conflict with each other, any one individual being a member of many identifiable groups. Without doubt, also, the resulting tendencies toward the development of some sort of pluralism are held in check by the strong bonds of joint interests which all members of the Soviet power elite have in common when they face the outside world and their own population. Moreover, we shall see below that some of the tendencies toward pluralism may have been checked, at least for the time being, by the Communist Party's resuming that sovereign position in Soviet society which it might be said to have lost between 1938 and 1953.*

Types of Social Control

Most Western political scientists would without hesitation describe the USSR as a totalitarian society. What the word *totalitarianism* means precisely is not at all clear. It came into vogue in the Western world after World War II, when the unspeakable inhumanities of the Nazi regime became a matter of public record. The term carries with it the notion of a regime's utter disregard of the dignity, feelings, and interests of its citizens. It reeks of the arbitrary and bloody police state, evokes nocturnal arrests and the concentration camp. Since then, some not very successful attempts have been made to refine the concept

* The detection of rival interest groups among the Soviet power elite and the analysis of jurisdictional struggles between them or between the Kremlin's leading personalities is a favorite pastime of Western scholars, journalists, and intelligence personnel. The methods employed by these "kremlinologists" are subject to very serious challenge. Painstaking and patient record keeping about the known facts concerning the careers of high bureaucrats, as exemplified by the works of John A. Armstrong and Boris Meissner, will yield some rewards when used with the utmost caution (see Boris Meissner and John Reshetar, eds., *The Communist Party of the Soviet Union,* New York, 1956, and John A. Armstrong, *The Soviet Bureaucratic Elite,* New York, 1959). Equally diligent probing into the esoteric code of communication used by the communist world can be crowned with considerable success, as proven by Myron Rush, *The Rise of Khrushchev* (Washington, D.C., 1958). Most statements made in the West about politics within the Kremlin, however, are based on irresponsible speculation about group loyalties and faction formation within the communist hierarchy. Some kremlinologists have such a thorough acquaintance with all available information about the communist world that even their speculations should be listened to with respect, even if they seem to be groundless. Such a writer is Boris I. Nicolaevsky, who publishes his shrewd guesses in the New York journal *Sotsialisticheskii Vestnik.* The bulk of such work, however, is of dubious value, including recent revelations by former high-ranking members of the Soviet Communist Party, such as Orlov and Avtorkhanov, whose writings seem to be based primarily on unreliable gossip.

and to portray totalitarianism as a unique phenomenon of our century. One of these attempts consists of the enumeration of certain essential features which together make up the totalitarian syndrome. When I use the term, I am thinking primarily of a society which attempts to control its citizens totally, a regime in which not the slightest degree of autonomy is conceded to individuals or groups, whatever their endeavor may be, a government which regards every human activity or pursuit as a matter of public policy. In this sense, the Soviet Union comes closer to the totalitarian model than any other modern society, although, with due allowance for technological differences, it can be argued that many societies of the past were governed according to similar totalitarian principles and manifested most if not all the essential traits of the totalitarian syndrome.*

* The term "totalitarianism" came into use in the English-speaking world only after World War II. Previously it had been used with pride by the German national socialists to describe the organizational principle of their party and state. After the defeat of Germany, the limitless brutality of the Hitler regime, which then became common knowledge, begged to be described by a new term, and totalitarianism came to be used for the purpose of describing what was thought of as a completely new form of government and social organization. Precisely what are the distinguishing traits of totalitarian regimes has not been made clear. Hannah Arendt's brilliant work on *The Origins of Totalitarianism* (New York, 1951) singled out a few features and traced their evolution but cannot be considered a satisfactory definition, especially since her knowledge of societies other than German was entirely inadequate. Her work implies that totalitarianism means the end of Western civilization, or indeed of all civilization. Since it erodes and finally causes the disappearance of all moral and rational standards, it heralds the coming of an unprecedented and irreversible barbarism. The definition given by Carl J. Friedrich and Zbigniew K. Brzezinski, *Totalitarian Dictatorship and Autocracy* (Cambridge, Mass., 1956) represents a more sober attempt to make what behavioral political scientists would call a model of totalitarianism. Their model, however, is open to many challenges in its details. See also Carl J. Friedrich (ed.), *Totalitarianism* (Cambridge, Mass., 1954) for additional contributions to an attempted definition of this "form of government."

There is little if anything in the lives and activities of Soviet citizens which the party does not regard as a matter of public policy and seek to manage or control—political activities; economic and professional performance; education and employment; both the production and enjoyment of entertainment, art, and all leisure activities; family life; ideas and beliefs, and even emotions, or at least their outward manifestations. In the eyes of many students, therefore, the Soviet system of government is characterized primarily by the universal urge to *control*, which they tend to derive from an insatiable urge to dominate; and this urge, in turn, is explained in many

My own belief is that Hannah Arendt is half right. The Soviet regime does indeed mean the end of an old civilization, and to those committed to it in all its detail, it may in fact look like the end of the world or the end of all human values. What she fails to realize is that out of all destructive revolutionary regimes, new orders have always emerged, incorporating a new ethos and reflecting human aspirations and human values in their special fashion. Like De Maistre or Burke, with whom she seems to sympathize, she can see only the loss that has been suffered.

A less passionate scholar would undoubtedly be able to see both the destructive and constructive processes and would therefore recognize the trends toward a new social order, even in the Soviet world. If indeed we must speak of totalitarianism, I would consider it useful to distinguish between at least two different types. One of them, associated with societies engaged in crash programs of industrialization, is characterized by the harsh features of Soviet rule during the reign of Stalin— police terror, superhuman work assignments, minimal rewards for most of the population, the ruthless eradication of preëxisting groups and traditions, and the use of human beings as an expendable resource. Another type of totalitarianism is associated with fully industrialized modern societies and is characterized by the bureaucratization of all endeavors, by the powerlessness of the individual, the rule of irresponsible elites wielding modern means of mass communication, creeping conformism, anti-intellectualism, and similar features. While both types have numerous traits in common, we should distinguish between them carefully. From my description it is obvious that, in my opinion, Soviet society is in the process of moving from the former into the latter form of totalitarian government.

different ways. In their writings, the attempt to establish total control at times becomes the very essence of the Soviet way of life, subsuming all other motives and relationships; and communist theory, too, is reduced to an organizational scheme designed to establish universal controls.[4]

Such a one-sided theory must be supplemented by additional explanations. A partial explanation lies in the fact that the economic goals of Soviet society (as defined by its power elite, to be sure) require a good deal of centralized planning and control. The relationship between economic goals and political systems, once the prime interest of students in political economy, has not in recent times received the attention it deserves. But it does seem clear that economic systems can be classified according to the goals to which they give priority, such as economic growth, equitable distribution (welfare state), the preservation of property rights, the most rational allocation of resources and perhaps others. If it is true that to every one of these goals a specific political structure is best suited, then undoubtedly centralization rather than decentralization, command rather than democracy, austerity rather than consumer sovereignty, seem to be designed to achieve rapid economic growth; and perhaps we might expect the attainment of this goal to open the way for a certain mellowing of the Soviet political system, a thesis expounded in recent years by Isaac Deutscher and some others.[5]

In subscribing to such an hypothesis, we need not be so naive as to suppose that the mellowing of the Soviet social system inevitably spells the emergence of constitutional democracy. Although such a development should not, perhaps, be dismissed as impossible, it seems far more likely, at this time, to assume that Soviet society will increasingly be characterized by a complex, pluralistic structure of interlocking bureaucratic hierarchies, perpetually straining under conflicting centralist and centrifugal tendencies, a unity containing ever increasing diversity. Again, in visualizing these trends of development, the model I have in mind is that of the giant Western corporation.

I should like to point out again, in this connection, that economic growth, or, more precisely, the rapid industrialization of a backward country, requires not only heavy capital investment and hence consumer austerity, which has to be forced upon people, not only centralized management, planning, and control of the economic machinery, not only add hard work from all citizens, from each according to his ability; it also requires that cultural revolution which Lenin demanded as early as 1922. And it is my belief that the exigencies of this concerted effort to transform a vast nation's entire way of life are as much responsible for Soviet totalitarianism as any other factor we have named. To be sure, Lenin said that the Soviet government must attempt to "build socialism" with the human material it found available in Russia. In fact, however, once the program of industrialization was started in earnest, the party tried to create the "new Soviet man," an individual well fitted to help in the effort to build and run a modern industrial establishment, a man equipped to live according to the rhythm of the machine rather than the rhythm of nature.

The methods used by the Soviet regime to control its population for these ends can be grouped in four main categories: rewards, sanctions, education, and organization.

Rewards. Chief among the rewards is organized inequality, according to the motto, "To each according to his work." In the USSR, the entire society is, as it were, earning piece-rate wages, sharply graded, with regressive taxation accenting the differences. Soviet society has been made rank conscious, for the rewards for top performance include deference made visible by uniforms, badges, titles, and similar tokens of status.

Equally important are the material benefits granted to all citizens regardless of performance. The USSR is a welfare state, in the sense that it strives to eliminate the most grievous hardships caused by disaster, disease, and old age, and tries to raise the material level of living for all.

The regime has at last begun to convince many of its citizens that the collective effort will result in material benefits for each individual, that unselfish work for little reward may therefore be no more than the rational pursuit of each individual's self-interest. Evidence of graft and high living among the power elite contradict this theory; but a majority of the population may nonetheless have accepted it. The steady improvement in the living standards, especially the improvement in social services such as education, medical help, and old-age security, have acted as powerful arguments in this direction. So also have the indications (of which most Soviet citizens are aware) that at last the USSR is showing herself capable of catching up with the West in industrial production and scientific achievement. The Soviet citizen is beginning to feel that he is a partner, albeit a lowly one, in a growing and successful enterprise. Several Western observers who have spent some time in the USSR seem prepared to say that this sentiment is particularly strong among the Soviet working class and that it leads to considerable job satisfaction. The Soviet worker genuinely seems to believe that he is working for himself, not just for his weekly pay envelope.

In addition, Soviet society is expanding, and the demand for talented and skilled personnel in every field seems insatiable. It is therefore a society with plenty of room at the top, not the very top perhaps, but certainly room in the top layer of experts and managers. Professionally, the USSR is a society wide open for young people with physical or intellectual endowment who are willing to work hard. Awareness of this undoubtedly attaches many of the younger generation to the regime.

Sanctions. Societies and cultures have not only different hierarchies of values but also different conceptions of the seriousness of deviant behavior. In modern societies, these conceptions are expressed by criminal law. Criminal law in the Soviet Union is designed to inflict harsh punishment on those citizens who refuse to contribute to the social construction effort in the prescribed manner.

Conformity to party standards is enforced, furthermore, by the extralegal terror of the political police. The aim of organized terror in the Soviet system is not so much to punish malperformance as to *prevent* heresy, dissent, or actions hostile to the regime. This is accomplished by keeping a continual check on all citizens' activities, associations, and environmental influences and by punishing those individuals or groups who on the bases of these influences can be expected to have open or latent tendencies toward disloyalty. Jerzy Gliksman has called this function of the terror "prophylactic justice." But even though this appears to be a very apt description of one of the tasks performed by the political police, it neglects another, equally important, one, which is that of serving as the eyes and ears of the regime in continually gauging the moods of the population. The secret police, in other words, functions as a public-opinion polling institution and in this fashion also helps to maintain controls. An incidental result of "prophylactic justice" was the use of prison labor on a very large scale in work projects for which, because of their difficulty or hazards or inhuman living conditions, it would have been hard to find volunteers. This notorious labor-camp system has been important in Soviet society since the early 1930's but has declined in recent years. Whether its decline is attributable to awareness that prison labor is inefficient is a matter of speculation. It could more simply be explained as a natural result of the marked decrease in the party's reliance on terror as a means of controlling the population. The party may no longer consider such drastic methods necessary; or else its leaders may have come to the conclusion that terror is too costly and too dangerous a means of control.

In recent years, the Soviet regime has experimented with sanctions wielded by peer groups of colleagues or neighbors, who are empowered to mete out summary punishment to persons unwilling to conform to Soviet standards of work or behavior. While this practice grossly violates Western notions of due process, the party has hailed it as one of the proofs that the state has begun to wither away.

Even if there were no terror whatsoever, the fact that the Soviet state is virtually the sole employer and educator makes all citizens highly dependent on the authorities and doubtless acts as an effective sanction against deviant behavior. The effectiveness of this hold of the monopolistic employer on the citizens may increase as the Soviet economy manages to replace human labor with automatic machines. Some observers of the Soviet scene already see the specter of technological unemployment looming over the horizon. So far, this is mostly speculation.

Education. Little needs to be said about education in the USSR. Entirely in the hands of the government, it is both a means of inculcating Soviet values and the party outlook in the younger generation and a method of structuring the labor supply and of screening personnel in all branches of activity. To the individual Soviet citizen, the educational system is a valuable social service provided without charge, which gives him an opportunity to move upward in the social scale, if he is not screened out by the very stiff selection process. What proportion of young citizens are aware that a strong bias distorts the information they receive; how many of them feel that *partiinost'* comes into conflict with science; or how many of them resent the tutelage exercised over their minds by the party—these are questions we cannot answer on the basis of available information.

Education is not confined to schools and universities. In the Soviet Union, as everywhere else, the media of mass communications—the press, radio, television—also function as educational institutions. Moreover, in the USSR, the entertainment media, too, have been made vehicles of the party's educational effort, and so have all other forms of communication, even literature and art, which are promoted and tolerated only as long as they carry the party's message to the masses. Whatever he may hear, see, or read, the Soviet citizen is thus likely to re-

ceive messages sent to him by the party with the aim of
making a more loyal and cooperative, a more "conscious,"
citizen of him. In short, all communications media in
Soviet society serve the purpose of frantic and relentless
indoctrination designed to make all citizens accept fully
and genuinely the values and goals of the political leadership. We have already indicated that, on the whole, the
party has been quite successful in thus socializing its
citizens.

Organization. Whatever the success of this unending
and inescapable educational effort, it could be achieved
only because all media of communication, from schools
to billboards, from the press to opera houses, are directly
or indirectly in the hands of the party. The party ensures
the success of its many efforts at indoctrination, control,
and management by wielding control over all the organizations within which the individuals carry on their various
activities.

In modern industrial societies everywhere fewer and
fewer functions are carried out by the isolated individual.
Instead, the functions of society are performed by organizations and associations, both formal and informal. The
founder of Russian Communism, Lenin, was one of the
first men to realize the political implications of this fact.
He seems to have realized that an elite dominating the
many organizations within which men play their social
roles could dominate the members. Organizations, said
Lenin, are transmission belts transferring to all members
the impetus given by the power behind the organization.
Organization is the tool by which men can be manipulated.*

Accordingly, the party in the USSR has attempted to
get hold of all organizations and associations, formal and
informal, constituting the society. It has done this with so
much success that the entire network of organizations
and associations in the Soviet Union is a huge and complex system of what we might call party front organiza-

* See Chapter 4.

tions. The process by which this organizational mastery
of society was achieved is akin to the *Gleichschaltung* of
German society undertaken by the national socialists after
coming to power. It is essentially a dual operation. The
first step is the destruction of all existing organizations
and associations which are not agencies of the party, from
rival parties through professional associations to youth
organizations and stamp collectors' clubs. In the Soviet
Union, much of this was accomplished in the period of
war communism; but the process was not completed until
about fifteen years after the revolution. Once it has been
accomplished, a new network of organizations can be
created by the party, in which all key positions are filled
by party members subject to party directives and discipline. The result of this reorganization (which began long
before the destruction of the old social structure was
completed) will be that many seemingly spontaneous
activities are in fact carried out under the planning, supervision, and control of the party. This, far more than
nighttime arrests and labor camps, is the essence of Soviet
totalitarianism.

Strains and Tensions

I have called the Soviet system a successful and growing enterprise, and I am sure that most observers would
agree with me in this judgment. Our awareness of the successes which Soviet communism has had in maintaining
and strengthening its economic system and social fabric
must not, however, cause us to neglect the strains in Soviet
society, of which we can list only the most important
here.

A very substantial amount of strain inherent in Soviet
society is the result of (mostly latent) hostility and resistance shown to the regime by the peasants. On a mass
scale, open resistance was offered last at the time of forced
collectivization, thirty years ago. Ever since then, the
peasantry has, most of the time, submitted to the regime.
But it has done so passively and sullenly. It has, despite

its submissive attitude, resisted both the party's attempt
to press a maximum of agricultural produce from the
kolkhoz system and the effort to educate and urbanize
the peasant, wean him away from religious beliefs and
make a conscious communist of him. The political education and the cultural revolution have not been spectacu-
larly successful in the Soviet countryside. This should not
astonish us; for, after all, the very meaning of the cultural
revolution was to stamp out the peasant way of life. It
is the peasant who is least adapted to the machine age
and its compelling rhythm; he who is most bound by religion and tradition; and he, too, who more fervently than
any other class yearns for private property.[6]

What applies to the peasant applies with even greater
emphasis to many of Soviet Russia's national minorities.
Not only are most of them overwhelmingly agricultural
in their occupation; some of them lived on an even more
primitive level of civilization than the Russian peasant,
so that the attempt to educate them to communism implies an even more thorough break with their traditional
way of life. In addition, the attempt to make the USSR
into a homogeneous industrial society necessarily led to
the imposition of the Russian language as an all-Soviet
lingua franca and to the encroachment of Russian personnel and Russian ways on the minority areas. Finally,
tendencies toward political independence or autonomy
have been stamped out ruthlessly wherever they appeared, often as a direct result of the cultural revolution.
All this makes some of the minority areas centers of latent
discontent and gives the party administrators something
of the character of colonial officials. And yet, while
there is some justification for comparing Soviet rule in
Asia with colonialism, it must be pointed out that this
colonial character of Soviet administration is bound to be
a passing phenomenon, for the USSR is doing its utmost
to industrialize the minority areas and integrate and ab-
sorb the minority peoples as quickly as possible.

The latent hostility against the regime is even greater
in those areas which, like the former Baltic republics,

are populated by minorities proud of their Western culture, who used to regard Russians as uncultured barbarians but must now learn to live as minorities within Communist Russia.

If the passive resistance shown by peasants, religious believers, and national minorities is a hangover from the pre-Soviet past, other loci of actual or potential discontent are the products of communist rule and industrial development. Foremost, and most general, among these is the silent resistance of large parts of the population against the sometimes impossible demands made on all individuals by the regime. This resistance takes many forms—apathy, alcoholism, and other forms of flight into deviant behavior, such as imitating Western styles of appearance or entertainment, and escape into illness, imagined, simulated, and even self-inflicted—but only rarely takes the more organized form of the strike, although occasionally one does hear about strikes in the Soviet Union. In the case of the responsible administrator, impossible or conflicting demands are countered by numerous evasive devices that seem to make a mockery of central planning and orderly, lawful procedure. Among virtually all citizens, it takes the form of a latent, but nonetheless persistent, dissatisfaction with the material austerity imposed on them by the regime, or, to put it differently, of consumer pressure for more adequate housing, clothing, food supplies, social services, and a general rise in the standard of living. Even though this consumer pressure does not take organized forms, the Soviet regime apparently shows a modicum of sensitivity to it.

Secondly, tension is created by the apparently growing resistance of professional experts in many fields against the eternal supervision and control by the party and the police. Soviet society, in other words, is not free of that conflict between professional and political considerations which plagues decision makers in other societies also. But in the Soviet Union this conflict is rarely allowed to come into the open; indeed, its very existence is denied because no possibility of conflict between professional and political considerations is acknowledged. Still, we receive increasing indications that economists, scientists, engineers, artists, lawyers, or professional soldiers make attempts to pit their own views against those of the party or simply to assert their professional autonomy. However feeble, this pressure amounts to a yearning for freedom of thought; and since the party has sought to incorporate all and any branches of knowledge into the ideology of Soviet Marxism, it is also a yearning for freedom to interpret or re-interpret Soviet dogmas. At times, the perpetual pressure for this freedom is carried even into such sensitive and openly political subjects as Marxist philosophy, history, or constitutional law; and the current preoccupation of the party leaders with the struggle against "revisionism" is in actual fact nothing else than a repudiation of the freedom of thought in these areas.

Revisionism, so-called, is dangerous to the party because any reinterpretation of Soviet dogmas might cause any number of Soviet intellectuals to pay renewed attention to certain elements of original Marxism which the party regards as inconvenient. Marxism is a liberational system of ideas. Again and again Marx stressed his absolute opposition to all social systems in which man is abused, dominated, exploited, or humiliated by his fellow men. This system of ideas has remained the Holy Writ in a society that incorporates domination and exploitation. It should not astonish us, therefore, that Marxist thought has a tremendous explosive potential, which every once in awhile is realized in individual Soviet citizens. That is why the party strives to maintain a tight monopoly on the right to interpret the Holy Writ and has transformed it into a dogmatic catechism designed to serve conservative functions. And yet, there are ever-recurrent tendencies to go back to the spirit of Marx, to criticize existing institutions in the name of Marxism and to press for the realization of the ideals it incorporates. These tendencies are the essence of what party ideologists call revisionism.

Postwar Developments and Trends

World War II strained every fiber of the Soviet social fabric. The population at large, the armed forces, and perhaps even the party, were unprepared for the German attack, and there was a good deal of demoralization. In the first few weeks, vast areas of territory and hundreds of thousands of troops were lost to the enemy. In some regions, particularly in the Ukraine and the Northern Caucasus, many greeted the German troops as liberators from the communist yoke, only to be disillusioned cruelly by the unspeakable barbarity of German rule in Russia.[7] As everyone knows, the war ended in the defeat of the Germans. But the Soviet Union bore the major brunt of it, and deep scars remained for many years. Millions of men had been lost, other millions maimed for life; countless villages, towns, and cities were razed; the grand effort toward rapid industrialization must have suffered serious setbacks affecting particularly the standard of living of the population.

During the war, the Soviet regime made a concerted effort to gain or maintain the loyalty of the entire population. For this purpose, the party de-emphasized specifically communist themes in its propaganda and stressed instead the ideas of patriotism. This war was to be a war for the defense of the native land rather than for the defense of communism. In line with this attempt to appeal to all Soviet people, the party opened its ranks to those who had distinguished themselves in battle; it tacitly tolerated peasant encroachments on collective farm property; it demonstratively made its peace with the Church; and by its alliance with the Western democracies it consciously or unconsciously instilled in many Soviet citizens the hope that after the war Soviet Russia would continue to collaborate with the democratic countries and that a more relaxed and a more prosperous life was in store for them.[8]

To curb these hopes, the party decided, once the war

had been won, to return to the sternest methods of economic, political, and ideological reconstruction. The party ranks were purged of many who had recently been admitted. Rigid consumer austerity and work discipline were enforced once more, and all ideas about ideological compromises or about future collaboration with the non-communist West were driven out of the heads of intellectuals with an iron broom. The ensuing campaign to purify Soviet doctrine and eliminate all deviators is often referred to as the *zhdanovshchina*, because Andrei Zhdanov, the head of the Leningrad regional party organization and a member of the Politburo, acted as its chief spokesman and inquisitor. But even after his death his policies were continued. As a matter of fact, the political atmosphere inside the country became even more tense in the late forties and early fifties, as additional deviators or presumed deviators were ferreted out, both in Russia and in the countries of Eastern Europe. By 1952 it appeared very much as if another major purge was being prepared in the highest levels of the party which would engulf Soviet society in a new reign of acute terror. Before these obvious preparations could bear fruit, however, the dictator of the country, Josef Stalin, died, in March 1953.

His death brought to the surface, at least temporarily, currents that had been hidden under the crust of his rule. One of these currents was the rivalry at the very top of the leadership group, possibly symbolizing a clash of group interests extending into the subordinate administrative layers. One of its first manifestations was the unsuccessful attempt by the police chief, Beria to seize power. It was followed by signs of a sharp rivalry between economic planners and managers, on the one hand, and the party *aktiv*, on the other; in this *aktiv* the balance of power seems to have lain in the provincial and regional party secretaries. Furthermore, there were some unsuccessful efforts by a few generals to make their weight felt in politics. The result of these political struggles appears to have been the ascendancy of N. S. Khrushchev as the new ruler of Soviet society, possibly as the spokesman or exponent of the party *aktiv*. In any event, the professional party administrators on the highest level appear to have regained the sovereign position within Soviet society which they had lost after 1938. Still, in the long run, the pluralistic tendencies within the Soviet power elite seem to have a good chance of corroding the sovereignty of the party, however slowly.[9]

A second current which came more into the open after Stalin's death was the yearning for professional autonomy and freedom of thought on the part of the educated. This yearning was expressed, albeit timidly, in many forms. There were ventures into new themes and a rejection of stereotyped formulas in novel writing and other forms of art. There were more open and more controversial discussions than previously about the relation between Marxism and various sciences. There was, and still is, a continual effort to reinterpret the history of the party and of Soviet society, with the result that Stalin has been denounced for having committed some mistakes; the great purges have been reëvaluated, and some of its victims have been rehabilitated. All in all, there were efforts in almost every field of activity and learning to release the intellectual ferment; and these efforts appear still to be going on, even though the party has repeatedly tried to bottle up the ferment. Here, too, the long-range trend is likely to favor the gradual corrosion of Marxist–Leninist dogmas and the growth of similarities between Soviet and American thinking and social processes. Already Soviet economists are employing Western planning concepts and are openly challenging the validity of basic Marxist ideas; while Soviet military strategists have, since 1955, rejected Stalinist dogmas in favor of Western principles of warfare. Similar processes of transformation are going on in many fields of endeavor.[10]

Since Stalin's death there has also been some relaxation of discipline, domination, and austerity. After the fall of Beria, the police was deprived of some of its arbitrary authority. Some of the "correctional labor" camps were dissolved. Attempts were made to bridge the social gap between the people and the rulers and also to draw the common man of Soviet society a little more into public life. While in the last years of Stalin's rule Soviet society was almost hermetically sealed off from all contacts with the non-Soviet world, the flow of communication between Soviet citizens and the outside resumed in the mid-1950's, through Western tourists, cultural exchanges, scientific collaboration, and the like.

Furthermore, Khrushchev's regime is marked by a significant decrease in the feverishness of indoctrination. Since much of the party ideology has been internalized by a sizable portion of the population, it has become like Sunday sermons or Fourth of July oratory. It is repeated ceremoniously and in stereotyped form for the purpose of upholding the regime's legitimacy, but it serves less and less as a guide to action. In fact, indoctrination, like police terror, is becoming a superfluous part of Soviet political behavior. Finally, a new party statute was adopted in the fall of 1961 which makes some initial concessions to the pressure for greater freedom of discussion and greater security of the individual party members.[11]

If these measures showed that the regime was more confident of success and of the loyalty of the people, it had good reasons. Not only had the USSR emerged as one of the two major world powers, whose leader was received in the White House, it had gained this world stature by spectacular military and scientific advances which few Westerners would have predicted ten years ago. Unlike the economic growth under the first and second five-year plans, progress was now accompanied by a rapid and steady rise in the standard of living for the entire population, and because of all this, vast masses of Soviet citizens must have gained greater confidence that they were part of a useful enterprise and that it would be to their self-interest to collaborate to the best of their ability. For the first time since the revolution of 1917, the regime seemed able to keep some of its promises.

10

World Communism since World War II

We live today in the most revolutionary of all ages. Major social transformations are going on in our lifetime which are more profound, more rapid, and more extensive than anything the history of mankind has seen. This revolution of our time is manifested in scientific, technological, political and cultural changes which by far transcend the topic of this little volume. But we can single out several changes that are directly related to the development of world communism since World War II.

The most conspicuous, perhaps, although by no means the most important, of these changes is the emergence of the Soviet Union as a world power, by virtue of her industrial growth, her scientific achievements, and her political successes. One of the consequences of this change in the international status of the USSR was that the international communist movement, too, acquired new strength, backed up as it now was by a strong power that could make its weight felt in world affairs. Not only did international communism acquire new strength; its meth-

ods, too, underwent significant changes. With the ability
of Soviet Russia to take the initiative in international affairs, and with the opportunities presented by the war for
moving into neighboring areas where power lay ready for
anyone who would pick it up, the Kremlin was given opportunities for making revolutions by armed conquest or
indirect international pressure, proletarian revolutions in
which the existence of native communist parties was less
important than the presence of Soviet troops and the overwhelming diplomatic strength of the Soviet government.
It is in this fashion that the communist governments of
Eastern Europe (with the exception of Yugoslavia) were
created. For the first time since 1917, viable communist
regimes had come to exist outside Russia, in societies different from that in which the bolsheviks had come to
power and where therefore the aims and methods of
government had to be different from those of Russia.
Since the spread of the revolution now coincided with the
extension of Soviet Russian national power, the persistent
conflict between the interests of the world revolution and
the national interests of the Soviet state tended to give way
to a merger of these interests.

A second feature of the revolution of our time is the
rapid disintegration of Western influence in the world
since World War II. For Central and Western Europe,
the war was a great disaster, causing vast destruction of
cities, economic disruption, and massive social unrest. As
a result, Europe definitely lost her position of leadership
in world affairs. The center of world power shifted from
London, Paris, and Berlin to Washington and Moscow.
But the war not only destroyed European hegemony; it
also gave a significant boost to a number of communist
parties. Wherever German occupation forces appeared,
be it in Greece or Estonia, Norway, France, or Italy, to
mention only a few countries, resistance movements came
into existence—guerrilla forces trying to harass German
troops, sabotage German communications, or prepare for
setting up governments of liberation. In these resistance
forces, communists took a very active part, being pre-

pared for such warfare by their underground experience and their political schooling. In many countries, they distinguished themselves by competent leadership and daring heroism. In Eastern Europe, especially in Poland and Yugoslavia, communist resistance forces fought bitterly against both the German or Italian occupation troops and noncommunist guerrilla units, whereas in the West the general pattern was a merger of all resistance forces under unified command, so that communists, socialists, and right-wing nationalists, atheists, and believers fought together. Throughout occupied territories, the communist parties derived considerable prestige from this activity and managed, after the war, to translate much of this prestige into political power, though in Western Europe they did not manage to hold on to this power. In any event, in the immediate postwar period one might say that the communist movement had achieved recognition as a respectable party whose representatives ought by rights to share government responsibility.

In East and Southeast Asia, in all areas occupied by Japan, very similar successes were won on the basis of participation and leadership in the resistance forces, and in many of these areas, the guerrilla activity meant the emergence of the communist party as a fully organized political force. Since instead of orderly government revolutionary civil war followed the defeat of the Japanese in many of these areas, political power in those cases meant the emergence of the communist party as a military force. The collapse of Japan gave some of the communist parties a substantial arsenal of enemy weapons with which to resume their revolutionary pursuits. A particularly rich harvest of arms was reaped by the communists in Manchuria, in the wake of Soviet military advances during the closing days of the war.

Foremost, however, the war spurred the colonial revolution to unprecedented intensity, creating new opportunities for communist revolutionary activity and giving the Soviet Union new occasions for interfering actively in world politics. If I have called ours the most revolutionary age of all history, I should assert also that the most spectacular element in this revolution of our time is the rise of the underdeveloped nations. When we study social sciences, we usually study the history, politics, and economics of Western Europe and North America. Our view of the world for centuries has been highly ethnocentric—and rightly so, for the nations of Asia, Africa, and Latin America did not count. However populous, they were negligible because of their political, economic, and military weakness. They were objects of exploitation or domination, either as colonies or as dependencies or satellites. The white man ruled these countries through unbelievably arrogant and arbitrary colonial administrators, military or civilian. Neither these officials nor the builders and traders and overseers who represented Western business were always the highest representatives of European civilization; on the contrary, service in the white man's underdeveloped dependencies often was sought by highly unattractive personalities, people who, as Hannah Arendt has put it, had become superfluous in their own societies.

The West, however, brought not only domination by tactless, stupid, or ruthless colonial officials, not only new forms of economic exploitation for native labor; it also brought blessings: material wealth through the implantation of Western industrial enterprises, valuable technical and administrative skills for a small elite of cooperative natives. For those blessings, the people of Asia, Africa, and Latin America are not, as a rule, grateful to the West. On the contrary, one legacy of colonialism and dependency is an unbounded hatred of the white man, who is remembered as the arrogant intruder, the tyrant, the barbarian, who disrupted and destroyed the traditional way of life and even claims gratitude for it.

Whatever the natives' attitude toward the West, there is one other thing which the white man's rule has brought to their countries; and that is revolution. Wherever they appeared, Western administration, Western commerce and industry disrupted old-established cultures, uprooting entire social classes. Christian missionaries meanwhile acquainted the natives with the idea of brotherly love, while Western educators sought to propagate democracy, free enterprise, nationalism, and socialism. With this education, the natives in underdeveloped and dependent countries were given various directions for solving the problems which the encroachment of the West had created for them. The lesson was that the colonial nations might improve their lot by applying Western ideas and ideals to their own societies.

The need for drastic action, for revolutionary transformation, which is felt by political leaders in underdeveloped areas is given its sense of urgency by the material misery of these countries. It has by now become common knowledge in the Western world that roughly two-thirds of the world's population exist on an average annual income of about fifty dollars per capita, a level of existence which Americans cannot even imagine. These figures spell starvation, disease, infant deaths, and short life spans on a gigantic scale, and in view of the population explosion which aggravates this misery there are no easy solutions. It might be argued that there is nonetheless no reason for the political leaders in Asia and Africa to become excited over the low standard of living in their countries, since, after all, this has been their condition for centuries. While this may indeed be true, there is one significant change: The world has today become a single political community. The various countries, industrial or preindustrial, no longer can lead a separate existence but become more and more aware of each other. Americans and Western Europeans, with their high standard of life, have become fellow citizens in this world community with starving Indians, disease-ridden Africans, and belabored South American peons, who therefore assume the character of underprivileged classes. Individuals in these classes may be illiterate and ignorant, and uninterested in sweeping political changes; but their spokesmen and manipulators are well aware of the unbelievable gap between the wealthy and the poor in this world community.

The solution most of these leaders advocate is westernization, that is, the adoption of the Western industrial way of life, the building of industries and cities, the training of the population for life and work in this environment, and the willingness to learn from Western experience in government and administration. Westernization, as advocated by revolutionary leaders in underdeveloped countries, must be seen as an act of revolt both against the old way of life and its representatives in the old ruling classes and cliques and against the West itself; for westernization is not only designed to modernize undeveloped countries and promote economic growth; it is also seen as a means of liberation and emancipation.

But what has all this to do with the development of communism? Merely because the colonial revolution is so clearly directed against the white man, we should not be so foolish as to characterize it offhandedly as a communist conspiracy. On the contrary, some of these revolutions would have happened earlier or been more successful had Moscow been more encouraging and cooperative, or more intelligent in its leadership. Indeed, in the eyes of many Asian or African revolutionaries communist Russia is as much a potential exploiter and oppressor as the former colonial masters; to them Russia is part of the West and bears a share of the guilt that is heaped on the West. But despite these reservations, Soviet Russia may be a desirable partner in economic construction for newly established regimes that might want to profit from Soviet economic aid and technical assistance or that might wish to extort such aid from the United States by parading their friendly dealings with Moscow. Beyond that, Soviet (and now also Chinese) communism is studied carefully by many revolutionary leaders in underdeveloped areas and exerts a strong attraction on them.

In their eyes, Russia is the first underdeveloped nation that has emancipated itself from Western influence and overcome its economic backwardness by a concerted effort, with spectacular success. When growth rates of the Soviet economy are contrasted with the business cycle in free-enterprise societies, the Soviet Union and China be-

come models for development, models that are the more
meaningful because ideals of democracy, individual freedom, and due process are not deeply rooted in many former colonial areas, especially where colonial administra-
tions have mocked them for decades; or they may be
considered luxuries which a backward nation cannot afford. Instead, the avowed elitism of the Soviet way of life
and the communist movement may appeal to revolutionary leaders in hierarchically ruled countries. In addition,
communist theory has features which make it well suited
to inspire such leaders. It is a sweeping theory of salvation
and damnation likely to make converts in violently disturbed societies and in times of dramatic revolutionary
upheavals. It is at least overtly an optimistic theory, which
asserts that progress is possible—again something which
seems almost deliberately designed to appeal to nations
emerging from preindustrialism. Moreover, in advocating
the machine age, although rebelling against Western
capitalism, communist thought very precisely expresses
the ambivalent attitude toward the West of people who
wish to westernize even while ridding themselves of Western rule. Finally, and perhaps most significantly, communist theory, in its ideas about imperialism, incorporates a
systematic theory of underdevelopment, and it is the first
and perhaps even the only theory which has attempted to
describe systematically the genesis and problems of
underdevelopment. The communists thereby have established a virtual monopoly on explaining the underdeveloped nations to themselves; hence the curious and slightly
disturbing phenomenon that spokesmen of such nations,
however violently anticommunist they be, almost inevitably use the language of Lenin when they begin to talk
about the economic problems of their countries. In this
fashion, then, the disintegration of Western influence is
at least indirectly related to the growth of communist
strength since World War II.

The Cold War

The revolution of our time, although an autonomous event, is yet connected in many ways with the cold war that has raged between the USSR and the USA for more than two decades. Seen in its narrowest perspective, this conflict is a dispute over the settlement of the last war; but it can also be regarded as an all-encompassing rivalry between the two superpowers for positions of strength and influence all over the world, and for the neutralization of the antagonist.

As early as 1943, once it had become apparent that the war was won, some party members in the Soviet Union were told confidentially that after the defeat of Germany the next enemy would be the United States. Still, in the subsequent years, the Kremlin appeared very reluctant to let any hostility against the West come into the open. Stalin seems to have believed for a number of years that he could ill afford to antagonize his former ally, the United States. This is the most plausible explanation of the fact that in this period Russia repeatedly discouraged or even hindered the attempts made by communist parties in France, Yugoslavia, China, and elsewhere to shift from a strategy of wartime alliance with "bourgeois" forces to one of open opposition and revolution. The only other explanation (and it may very well have been true as well) is that Stalin no longer cared for the promotion of communist revolutions unless he himself, or his direct subordinates, could plan and supervise them. Thus, while communist parties outside of direct Soviet control were forced to collaborate with groups whom in reality they wished to dislodge (in Yugoslavia, let us note, Stalin did not succeed in forcing the party to adopt this line), Soviet activity in the conquered or liberated countries of Eastern Europe was designed to ensure the transformation of their governments into purely communist regimes.

The Soviet advance into Eastern Europe began in September 1939, when on the basis of her recent agreement with the Third Reich the USSR annexed the eastern half of Poland. Supported by the same treaty, she added the three Baltic republics as well as parts of Finland and Rumania the following year. All these territories were lost again to the Germans in 1941, but Moscow kept claiming a legal right to them; and her new allies in the West did not consider it opportune to challenge these claims openly. Moreover, the wartime governments of Britain and the United States considered themselves so dependent on continued Soviet cooperation that in their agreements with Stalin they conceded to him overriding influence in all of Eastern Europe except Greece. Provisions guaranteeing the independence and democratic nature of the postwar regimes to be set up in Eastern Europe were left deliberately vague. In effect, therefore, the Western powers allotted or sold these countries to the Russians; they thought at the time that such a deal was inevitable.

If Stalin was thus given a fairly free hand in transforming Eastern Europe according to the Soviet image, the local communist parties were aided by a number of additional circumstances. Their record in the resistance movements gave them prestige and a claim to a share in power. The old ruling classes had been decimated by the occupation or stigmatized as collaborationists; their parties had dwindled or were outlawed; their property had been taken over by the Germans and, after liberation, was often retained by the new governments as being enemy property. Many people in Balkanized Eastern Europe, moreover, were weary of bloody conflict between national minorities, and some of them may have been impressed with the Soviet solution of this problem. In some of the Eastern European countries, finally, age-old feelings of brotherhood for the Russians had been reawakened and could be exploited by the communists. There were thus, in spite of widespread hatred or fear of the Russians or of communism, many factors which predisposed many people in this area to accept socialism and collaborate with the communists. Nonetheless, the transformation of Eastern Europe into a set of purely communist regimes had to be done by a combination of stealth and force, utilizing all the advantages which the communists possessed by virtue of the Soviet army's presence. The transformation was, on the whole, well managed and was accomplished in less than four years. By the spring of 1948, all governments in Eastern Europe were in essence communist dictatorships. Although formally these regimes were governed by parties with a broader following and a more diffuse ideology than communist parties, for practical purposes these coalition parties were full-fledged communist parties. By means of thorough purges and other less bloody maneuvers, Stalin managed to place every one of these parties under the command of men absolutely loyal and obedient to him, little Stalins themselves, who faithfully followed every cue Moscow gave them and ruthlessly enforced their commands through means of government tested in the USSR. Party dictatorship, police terror, forced collectivization, economic centralization, consumer austerity, and the strictest control of all human activities came to characterize the regimes of Eastern Europe, while, in turn, Moscow maintained its own control over them by a variety of methods. In the ten years following the end of World War II, communist government in Eastern Europe resulted in rapid industrial growth and equally rapid social dislocation—a scrambling of society which, in the short run, gave rise to tremendous tensions and dissatisfactions, especially among the urban workers and intellectuals, but which, in the long run, was doubtless designed to make communist government more acceptable to these nations. The undeniable success of the regimes in transforming their countries in the Soviet image and raising them to the level of industrial nations was marred, however, by several factors: Soviet economic exploitation robbed them of much of the fruits of their labor; economic growth was perverted by strong strivings for autarky, which were encouraged by the Kremlin; and, finally, these strivings for self-sufficiency were part of a surprising amount of national antagonism between the various Eastern European regimes.

The transformation of the Eastern European countries into communist regimes has increased the military and economic strength of the communist world and has given it added weight in the community of nations. But it has also created problems for the communists—political as well as ideological ones. Among the communist leaders who acquired power in Eastern Europe after the war, there were many who, despite their devotion to the movement and to Soviet Russia as its center, were hopeful that some of the harshest features of the Soviet way of life might be avoided in their own countries. The low living standard and the unyielding dictatorship of the communist bosses, the reign of the police and the general disregard for the happiness of individuals and groups, the lack of intellectual freedom and the hermetic isolation of Soviet citizens from the outside world—these and other features were explained as necessary consequences of Russia's backwardness. In countries like Czechoslovakia, Poland, Hungary, and East Germany, where an industrial base already existed, where the old ruling class had been wiped out or discredited, and where socialism was generally accepted as inevitable if not desirable, many native communists sincerely believed that something like a democratic or at least more humane type of communism could be developed and that the Soviet pattern of development need not necessarily be followed in all its details. In short, the Kremlin's effort to force the Eastern European regimes to adopt Stalinist methods of "building socialism" came into conflict with the obvious fact that the nations of that area lived under circumstances differing from those in the USSR. They lived by different intellectual traditions and on different levels of economic and social development. These differences were acknowledged, at least temporarily, even by the Kremlin high command and found reflection in various doctrinal adjustments. For instance, the communist regimes of Eastern Europe were not designated as soviet republics and, for the time being, refrained from describing themselves as dictatorships of the proletariat. Instead, they called themselves "peo-

ple's democracies," and the official explanation of this new
term in the communist catechism made clear that the establishment of people's democracies spelled a coalition of
parties and classes some of which were still features of
the capitalist past; moreover, the fact that the countries
of Eastern Europe were not incorporated in the Soviet
Union was an explicit concession to the strength of nationalism in that area. Despite such doctrinal adjustments,
however, the actual governing of the Eastern European
countries was more similar to the Soviet pattern than
was acceptable to many of their political leaders, including some communists.

It is ironic that the man who became the spokesman
for such protest views was the one Eastern European
leader who harbored the greatest reservations about them.
Marshal Tito, the ruler of Yugoslavia, was the most loyal
Stalinist of all the postwar leaders of Eastern Europe and
the least sympathetic to the "revisionist" views of some
of his colleagues in neighboring countries. Circumstances,
however, caused him to quarrel with his colleagues in
Moscow, and when he stood his ground, he unexpectedly
found himself labeled a heretic and an outcast from the
communist fold, a traitor to the revolution and an agent
of imperialism. Once in this position, he was bound,
though only very gradually and cautiously, to justify his
status ideologically. Consequently, his regime began to
express systematically some of the disappointed hopes of
Eastern European communists. Moreover, many communists in Western countries seem to have been inspired by
the notion of communism without some of the most ob-
noxious features of Soviet rule—an autonomous, polycen-
tric, humane, perhaps even democratic communism. The
stirrings in Eastern Europe and the successful resistance
to Moscow of Tito were thus echoed by lively debates and
a good deal of soul searching among communists and
their sympathizers in Western Europe and North America, who now envisaged a non-Russian alternative to Stalinism.

In Eastern Europe, the yearning for more moderate

methods was without doubt based primarily on an awareness of the sharp tensions and dissatisfactions created by
communist policies. The aim of the "revisionists" was to
ease the tensions and alleviate the dissatisfaction. Very
likely the tougher-minded "Stalinists" who won over them
temporarily were just as much aware of the underlying
difficulties. But, instead of giving way to popular sentiment, they doubtless hoped to overcome these difficulties
by suppressing them and thus all the more rapidly transforming society in the communist image. In other words,
they were intent upon allaying dissatisfaction and unrest
through industrialization and collectivization. Eastern
European communism thus found itself engaged in the
same great debate which shook the Russian Communist
Party during the period of the New Economic Policy.

This time, the conflict was solved, for the time being,
with the help of the Kremlin. While it may have seemed
implausible at the time to assume that Eastern European
revisionist ideas constituted a threat to the Soviet Union,
Stalin took vigorous action to suppress all such notions.
He may have had any or all of the following reasons for
his intolerance. He may have realized more clearly than
Western observers that these ideas could produce open
rebellions such as those which occurred in Germany,
Czechoslovakia, Poland, and Hungary in 1953 and 1956.
He may also have worried about the impact which the
development of some sort of democratic communism anywhere might have had on his own Russian population: if
the Poles and the Czechs had been granted more freedom
and a higher standard of living, the Soviet people might
have demanded the same. In addition, distrust of autonomy and the urge to control and coordinate is endemic in
the communist system of government. It so happened,
moreover, that unorthodox ideas of this kind were particularly popular among communists who had fought in resistance movements in their own countries or who had
spent the war years in exile in the West. The Russians,
apparently, did not trust such communists and sought to
replace them by faithful organization men who had spent

the war years and perhaps more in the Soviet Union, who may even have weathered the great purges of the 1930's and were known as loyal and safe. The principal reason, however, which compelled Stalin to suppress the revisionists was the fact that he did not care to permit the people of Poland, Czechoslovakia, and other countries possessing an industrial base to benefit from this higher economic development. Instead, he wanted to divert a maximal share of the products of these countries to the USSR, for the sake of reconstructing his own ravaged country and raising the living standard of his own population. This policy implied the drastic imposition of an austerity regime in the Eastern European satellites, together with pressures for harsh work discipline and totalitarian conformity, dashing the hopes for autonomy and democratic communism. But despite these efforts, heretical beliefs and hopes never did perish among the communists of Eastern Europe. And in subsequent years, their heresy was to present the Soviet Union with grave political problems, with which we shall deal further below.

Moscow's fight against the heresy of revisionism began in earnest before the defection of Tito (1947), though it became a bloody purge only in subsequent years. The creation of the Communist Information Bureau (Cominform) in 1947 appears to have been a move toward keeping the parties of Eastern Europe and those of France and Italy in line. In other ways, too, Moscow put its foreign comrades on notice that the conflict with the former allies, especially with the United States, had broken into the open. The purge of Earl Browder from leadership of the American Communist Party (he too had advocated a sort of autonomous communism) is as much part of this development as the denunciation of the Soviet economist Varga, who had attempted to demonstrate that the American economy would survive the difficulties of converting to peacetime production; or the fight against "rootless cosmopolitans" among Soviet intellectuals, who dared to maintain contact with their Western colleagues or even to acknowledge that Western achievements in science or art merited any attention whatsoever. The cold war was on. It was from the beginning an anti-American political operation. America was denounced as the heir of imperialism and the center of a world-wide conspiracy to involve the world in a new war, with the capitalists of Wall Street pulling the strings that made reactionary politicians all over the world dance obediently. Against this Wall Street conspiracy to dominate or destroy the world and annihilate the constructive gains of Soviet socialism, Moscow appealed to numerous forces and groups that might be alarmed into opposing America. In underdeveloped countries, the USSR gave open or silent support to communist parties and military units, such as the armies of Mao Tse-tung and Ho Chi-minh and the guerrilla troops of Malaya. It denounced all those political leaders who declared themselves uninterested in the cold war, who wanted to form a neutral Third Force. Preoccupied with the specter of American aggression, Moscow denounced all noncommunist forces on the principle that "whoever is not unconditionally with us is against us." This spirit of exclusiveness made it impossible for the Kremlin to take full advantage of the revolutionary stirrings in the underdeveloped nations and may even have caused Moscow to be overly cautious in giving support to the communist parties of China, North Korea, and Northern Vietnam, in their march to victory. Noncommunist support was sought only for limited defensive or diversionary operations, such as the peace and disarmament campaign, in which everywhere war-weary people from all walks of life were urged to join the protest against atomic armament (the United States still had a monopoly of such weapons at that time). The culmination of the cold war came with events that were not instigated directly by the Soviet Union but undoubtedly received help and encouragement: the Chinese Revolution, the Korean War, and the war in Indochina. After that, there came a period of stalemate.

The balance sheet of these years shows some spectacular successes and some important failures for world communism. In addition to Eastern Europe and North Korea, the whole of continental China had been added to the communist bloc, and the northern half of Vietnam was added some years later. The Korean War, however, had ended in a draw, and in Europe there had been setbacks. The defection of Yugoslavia had created a serious gap in the phalanx of Eastern European satellite governments, the communist parties of Italy and France had been eliminated from the coalition governments they had entered after the war. Berlin remained a Western outpost and a thorn in the flesh of the East German communist rulers. On a world-wide scale, the United States committed herself with some determination to the policy of "holding the line" and organized her allies in a number of defensive blocs that created a ring of military bases around the entire communist world. At least for the time being, the front lines hardened.

Stalin's death in March 1953 brought with it a slight relaxation of tension. The "breaking of the ice" (usually translated as the "thaw") noted by Soviet intellectuals made itself felt also in international affairs: while still stressing the basic incompatibility between capitalist and communist goals and methods, the leaders of the communist world gave new stress to the themes of peaceful coexistence, constructive competition, and an easing of tensions. Within the communist camp, Moscow showed some toleration of revisionist or autonomist heresies in Eastern Europe; in these countries, too, doctrinal discipline was relaxed somewhat, and the Eastern European regimes were allowed to experiment with administrative or economic methods hitherto prohibited. The emergence of a communist China had already made it necessary for Moscow to make allowances for differences in method and ideology, if only by implication; for with Mao Tsetung and Chou En-lai men had come to power who were the equals, not the subordinates or creatures, of the rulers in Moscow. By 1955, Moscow had extended the principle that socialist development may take different forms to

Yugoslavia. The dissolution of the already moribund
Cominform in 1956 was merely a symbol of this rap-
prochement between Moscow and Belgrade.

About the reasons for this relaxation we can only spec-
ulate. It may be that Stalin's lieutenants, insecure in their
leaderless position, wished to secure the loyalty of their
constituents. Some students think they can detect in prerevolutionary Russian history a recurrent pattern of relaxation and concessions after the death of each tsar, and
they place the policies following Stalin's death in this pattern. Others argue that the new leaders were so preoccupied with the struggle for power among themselves that
they could not exert as tight a control over Soviet society
as the late dictator, and that the reimposition of such
control had to wait until a new dictator had installed himself. Again, there is some indication that the new leaders
had convinced themselves that Stalin's ruthlessness and
inflexibility had led to a stalemate, and that the governing
of the more mature society which Russia had become
called for more enlightened methods. Some Kremlin leaders undoubtedly were swayed by the logic of atomic and
nuclear warfare, which demands accommodation and
compromise and makes truculence a suicidal attitude.
Finally, after Stalin's death the Eastern European regimes
began to be troubled by a good deal of restiveness and dis-
order. Beginning with more and more open expressions
of discontent and disillusionment by hitherto loyal communists, this widespread restiveness at times erupted into
open uprising—a spontaneous revolt in East Germany in
June 1953, which was sparked by a workers' demonstra-
tion and had to be put down by Soviet military forces; a
serious strike during the same year in Plzeň, Czechoslovakia; the Poznań riots in the summer of 1956 and the general ferment following these disorders; the subsequent
defiance shown by the Polish communists to the Soviet
emissaries after the reinstatement of the "revisionist"
Gomulka as party chief; and, finally, the Hungarian uprising of October 1956. These acts of defiance not only con-

tradicted the conviction current among most scholars that there was no possibility of revolt against communist totalitarianism; they also demonstrated to the Eastern European communists the shakiness of their regimes. For the people who had led all these revolts, at least in the beginnings, had been either workers—the class considered most loyal and reliable by the communists—or communist party members and leaders, who had encouraged the expression of criticism and prepared political changes. This certainly was the case in both Poland and Hungary. In both countries the party leadership was openly divided, and the advocates of reform and relaxation defeated the "conservative" Stalinists. In Poland they were able to make their victory stick, win a number of concessions from the Russians, rid themselves of some of the leaders whom Moscow had imposed on them, and institute several reforms in their own country designed to satisfy or appease the peasantry, the church, small independent businessmen, or the population as a whole. Very similar measures were begun by the Hungarian regime, but the reform movement got out of hand and turned into open revolution, which was then bloodily suppressed by Soviet troops. Both before and after this dramatic event, almost all of Eastern Europe's communist regimes, in varying degrees, relieved their citizens of some of the pressures previously imposed on them; and the USSR, in turn, appears to have made economic concessions to its satellites.

While the unrest in Eastern Europe may have been one of the causes for the post-Stalin relaxation of pressure, the brutal suppression of the Hungarian uprising seems to mark the end of a period of concessions and to have ushered in a new period of aggressiveness in domestic and international affairs. In actual fact, concessions continued to be made, and the years since 1956 have yielded a rather contradictory pattern of communist behavior.

Unity and Diversity in Contemporary Communism

The growing disunity and diversity within contemporary communism is in sharp conflict with the popular image of communism in the Western world. Here we have come to see communism as an entirely undifferentiated bloc, a monolith which is well defined and uniform. We think of communist ideology as a matrix of ideas, a firm operational code yielding school solutions to its initiates, a master plan for world domination executed by a diabolically cunning intelligence. Some of us think of communist policies as flowing directly from this operational code and therefore consistent and unambiguous.

In trying to destroy this false image, I have no wish to deny that communist ideas have certain fixed themes to which all communists subscribe. If there were not some broad syndrome of attitudes or cluster of concepts which all communists have in common, this little volume should not have been written. Even today, all communists agree in general that the contemporary world should be seen in terms of Lenin's theory of imperialism. According to this theory, free enterprise and free trade have long ago yielded to the rule of national and international monopolies and to a growing tendency toward state capitalism, the state itself having become the tool of the monopolists. In this capitalist world, one nation, the United States, has become dominant and has reduced the other capitalist countries to satellites who dare rebel against the commands of Washington only rarely, even though many of their citizens resent their governments' subservience to America. In world affairs, the bloc of capitalist states, allied with the most reactionary tyrants in underdeveloped nations, is fighting, with the utmost ruthlessness, a desperate rear-guard action to preserve its political and economic investments in dependent areas against the onslaught of native democracy. In order to divert the people's attention from capitalist misrule and exploitation, moreover, the imperialists without cease use their favorite device of slandering communism, blaming it for all evils in the world and preparing war for the destruction of the socialist countries. Under the pretext of being threatened by communism, the imperialists mobilize their populations and pervert bourgeois democracy into the open dictatorship of the garrison state. Meanwhile, out of selfish commercial and evil political motives, the cultural heritage of the West has been squandered, yielding to the barbarism of nonobjective painting, Coca-Cola, and rock-and-roll, to the reign of gangsters and the preoccupation with sex. This, in brief, would be a summary of the way in which communist theory today describes the Western world.

Furthermore, all communists agree that the world today is divided into two main camps, the capitalist and the socialist, and that all countries belonging to the latter have certain interests in common. Even this has by now become an overstatement, since the communists of Yugoslavia, unsuccessful in their attempts to remain members of the Soviet bloc, have returned to their policy of "active neutralism," thereby indicating that, in their country at least, the building of socialism may place them in conflict with the "socialist camp" dominated by the USSR. Moreover, as we shall see, even within the socialist camp, there is today a growing trend toward a diversification of institutions and methods of "building socialism."

As for the view of the capitalist world, within the general agreement there are a number of important controversies. One area of disagreement is the correct assessment of the mood of the working class in Western society. Here the controversy appears as a conflict between theory and practice. In theory, the communist world expects the Western proletariat to sink into greater and greater misery and to rise up in revolt to expropriate the capitalists. This belief, often shaken by events, was not repudiated for several decades and is still being regarded as dogma by many communists, even though it is not clear whether they in fact believe it. As early as the 1920's, Bukharin tried to convince the Comintern that the hopes for proletarian revolution in the West were without foundation because imperialist capitalism had managed to "organize itself." He was sharply repudiated at the time by Lenin and, later, by his successors. But the Khrushchev school of communism seems finally to have accepted it. In practice, all of world communism appears to have given up hope of a Western proletarian revolution; and the proof of this is the insignificance of communist parties in the West. Communist parties in most Western nations are minute sects without even the hope of exerting mass appeal. This is true in the Anglo-Saxon countries and in Northern Europe as well as in most of the Mediterranean countries. It has, up to now, been true also in Latin America, although careful work and generous expenditures may have created a strong communist movement in at least some nations there. Moreover, revolutionary movements characterized by fierce nationalism, anti-Americanism, and some vague commitment to socialism seem to be rapidly increasing in Latin America. North America, in contrast, seems to have developed such strong intellectual antibodies that communist parties play no significant role. Although legions of policemen are making their living by keeping communists under surveillance, communists present no serious threat to the West and cannot play an important role in the plans of world communism, wherever such plans may be coordinated.

Strong communist parties exist today in only two Western nations, France and Italy, where about 20 and 30 per cent, respectively, of the voters have, since the war, voted for the communists. In France, this vote is not always reflected in the number of deputies elected to parliament, because electoral laws are deliberately rigged so as to exclude communists from elected office. The wartime experience which led to the renascence of these parties, and the experience of sharing power with other parties in the years immediately following World War II, have not only strengthened French and Italian communism; they have also changed and corrupted it. The Communist Party in Italy, if not in France, has become a patronage party interested in the immediate fruits of office for its functionaries. In both countries, communist strength is rooted primarily in the trade-union movement, which fell under party domination during or after the war; but this, to-

gether with the experience of office holding in local and
regional posts, has given the parties a preoccupation with
bread-and-butter questions which Lenin condemned as
"trade-unionist." In addition, the communists have to
compete with other socialist parties for the allegiance of
the workers and other voters; and this competition has
tended to drive them further and further to the right in
their policy statements. The parties, in short, concentrate
on issues and goals that have nothing to do with communism and are thus being assimilated to the domestic political scene, being tamed and absorbed. They fight within
the present social and economic system, not against it.
Typically, both in Italy and France the communist parties
try very hard to identify themselves with national revolutionary traditions, with the national political and ideological heritage; and their spokesmen are beginning to sound
like old-fashioned 19th-century radicals. To be sure, they
roundly criticize the existing regimes and predict their
overthrow by proletarian revolutions. They receive the
votes of those citizens who feel that they are getting an
unfair deal and want to protest against the established
order. The communist parties in Italy and France are protest parties. But this very function militates against revolution. By protesting, by threatening with the doom of
revolution, they obviate the necessity of seriously preparing such a revolution. Being the permanent opposition,
they only perpetuate the permanent disfranchisement of
the workers and the poor peasants, a political relationship
which itself has become traditional in France and Italy.
It becomes apparent here that the communist parties of
these two countries have become the heirs or successors
of the once-powerful (and yet ineffectual) social-democratic movement, which by now has become a shadow of
its former self. The communists' avowed policy is to defend the exploited, to save democracy, and to prevent a
third world war—a clear commitment to a "menshevik"
minimum program. Their method is the United Front
with other left-of-center groups, an alliance which in reality is impossible as long as the political system functions

tolerably well and which is unnecessary when it does not. Besides this, the communist parties have only the eternal function of acting as shield, salesman, and possibly as the intelligence agent of Soviet Russia and other communist states; and where there are other socialist parties, the communists cannot be distinguished from them by greater revolutionary fervor but only by their unquestioning loyalty to the USSR. Even this has at times been shaky, especially in Italy, where Togliatti for a while came out in favor of "polycentrism." For this reason, crises in the two parties are most often provoked by unpopular action taken by Moscow, such as the armed intervention in Hungary. At the same time, any tendency toward relaxation in Moscow is likely to strengthen Revisionist tendencies in the communist parties of Eastern and Western Europe.[1]

The trade-unionist character of the Western communist parties not only implies a conflict between theory and practice; it also spells a profound difference in the personnel and following of various communist parties. And yet, the difference between the Italian and the Czech communist, to name two at random, would be even greater if the Italian party were truly radical and revolutionary, if its goal were the liberation of the workers rather than their better accommodation within the existing system. For were radical criticism and the idea of liberty alive in the Western communist parties, it would be difficult for their followers to identify their fate with that of the Soviet Union to the extent they have done in the past. Conversely, it is precisely because they learned to be subservient to Moscow that the Western communist leaders could accommodate themselves to the opportunism and trade unionism, the patronage seeking and lack of radicalism they have shown since the war.

A second point on which there is no clear agreement among communists is the aggressiveness of the West. Communist policy has for decades been based on a theory of containment, which took it for granted that capitalism must seek the destruction of socialist states. This clear and ever-present danger of capitalist warmongering has been one of the cornerstones of communist theory. It took the form of the Leninist assumption of the inevitability of war, as long as capitalism was not destroyed. But in recent years, the Russian leaders have pointed to countertrends within the capitalist world, such as the disagreements among Western governments and the yearning for peace on the part of the people. Moreover, recent Soviet scientific and military achievements have so changed the balance of military potential that many Soviet leaders may be confident that at least they can curb Western aggressiveness by the deterrent of their retaliatory power.[2] Certainly Khrushchev's pronouncements have established a Soviet policy of containment through nuclear deterrent. In his speech in Bucharest, in June 1960, Khrushchev quite clearly repudiated Lenin's theory of the inevitability of war and maintained that there no longer was any alternative to peace. With their open neutralism, Marshal Tito and Imre Nagy went further than that; and so did the Polish Foreign Minister, Rapacki, in his proposals for disengagement in Central Europe. This stand in favor of coexistence is roundly opposed by communist leaders in China, Albania, and several other countries of Asia and Latin America who insist on the inevitability of war and the impossibility of long-range coexistence with capitalism and criticize Khrushchev's amendments of Leninism as outright betrayal. As Brzezinski has pointed out, Mao and his friends are quite correct; for Khrushchev's new line, according to which the communist camp can now relax a bit because the enemy is licked sufficiently and can now be contained—this line is essentially the position adopted by the Russian mensheviks vis-à-vis tsarist autocracy after the revolution of 1905. Khrushchev (not to speak of Tito, Gomulka, and others) has thus become the heir of the mensheviks and is fought by Mao and others with the same arguments Lenin used fifty years ago: while Khrushchev and his associates stress coexistence and the inevitability of gradual gains, Mao and his comrades insist on the continuation of the class struggle, and they agree with Marx that no significant changes ever take place in human society without the application of violence.[3]

The controversy over coexistence is related to disagreement regarding the viability of the Western social system, the ability of capitalist society to solve the problems posed by the twentieth century. Communists pay less attention than Western political scientists to the muddle and chaos of the free-enterprise political process, being satisfied, in general, with seeing the ubiquitous hidden hand of monopoly control behind everything that takes place. Instead, they look at the economic system, and here they seem to be undecided. On the one hand, their theory tells them that capitalism, even in its imperialist phase, cannot survive for long. Every recession confirms this belief; and it is further supported by the assumption that only extensive spending for armaments continues to prop up the Western economies. Undoubtedly, one of the several motives behind Soviet disarmament proposals is the hope that sweeping disarmament will cause crippling dislocation in the Western economic system. On the other hand, most communist leaders probably recognize and respect the scientific and economic achievements as well as the military might of the West. They are not likely to have illusions that this strength might be undermined very suddenly, despite recessions and the threat of disarmament. Although in 1947 Professor Varga was censured for predicting the survival of the American economy, we see that similar opinions are nonetheless still alive and have again been expressed by Soviet economists. Thus again, some of the communist leaders seem to be prepared for a prolonged era of coexistence; and, while they still maintain the inevitability of socialism, this belief in peaceful coexistence is connected with a belief that, in some places at least, the revolution will be a peaceful process. Here too affinities with menshevism are apparent; and the belief in the possibility of a peaceful transition to socialism is therefore called social democratism.[4]

That the role to be played by the proletariat or the communist parties in the West is negligible we have seen.

If revolution is to be promoted at all, it will therefore be the colonial revolution. According to Lenin, the emancipation of formerly dependent nations would lead to the crumbling of imperialism and would therefore be an important auxiliary force for world communism. Colonial revolutions are to be supported and promoted. While the communist movement subscribes to this in theory, Moscow's record of achievement is not spectacular. True, the colonial revolution today is engulfing large parts of the globe. But it is doubtful whether the contributions made by the communists have great significance. In Southern Asia, Equatorial Africa, and Central America the communists have played minor roles almost without exception. They give encouragement; they seek to participate; they may derive advantages from revolutions that have been accomplished; and increasingly they give economic or military aid and political support to successful revolutionary regimes. In isolated areas, they have shown considerable strength and have either assumed power or shared power in coalition governments. Thus they are present in every upheaval as potential beneficiaries. But they have not caused or even significantly speeded up any revolutions. The reasons for this are, first, that for about ten years after the end of World War II the Russian communists were too doctrinaire in their attitude toward revolutionary parties and therefore gave support only to their own creatures or loyal followers—a self-defeating attitude for exploiting unprecedented revolutionary situations. In turn, this doctrinaire exclusivism may have been, among other things, a cloak for timidity and caution, for Stalin's unwillingness to commit Soviet resources in support of revolutionary ventures throughout the globe.

Within the Kremlin today there is an obvious conflict between those "conservative" spokesmen who still would give secondary importance to the colonial revolution—either because they do not trust anyone but Moscow-trained communists, or because they are loath to commit precious resources for unreliable ventures, or else because they are preoccupied with the Cold War against America

—and those who propose to engage in peaceful competition with the West for the allegiance of the uncommitted areas and who therefore favor coexistence, disengagement, and foreign aid to underdeveloped nations. This is a conflict similar to the one between Cold War die-hards and foreign-aid advocates in the West; and it divides not only the Soviet leadership but also the communist world as a whole, just as the great debate about Western policy is carried out not only within any one country but also between various Western governments.

Communist disagreements over the nature of contemporary capitalism and over the best method for spreading the revolution are related to even sharper divergences, theoretical and practical, in regard to the nature of the socialist states already established. It must have become clear to the reader that the governmental practices of the various communist states, from Yugoslavia and Poland to North Korea and China, could not be fitted into the same mold of institutions and doctrines. By slow and painful adjustments, therefore, communism has come to recognize "different roads" toward socialism. Such adjustments are still being made and are still being resisted in a running debate that has been going on since the end of the war and will doubtless continue for some time.

The old Stalinist pattern was to enforce uniformity of methods, institutions, and doctrines throughout the socialist camp. Stalin's aim, as indicated above, was to suppress Eastern European communists who demanded the right to travel their own road toward socialism. Today, this effort has broken down, and a number of different types of communist governments have come to coexist. Let us briefly survey the Yugoslav, the Polish, and the Chinese variants, with some general observations about other Eastern European regimes. We shall begin with Yugoslavia.

Titoism can be reduced to a few simple formulas. It contains, first of all, the insistence that every country must go its own way toward socialism, the belief that local conditions and customs must be taken into consideration in mapping communist strategy both before and after the assumption of power. With this demand for an autonomous communism, Tito, consciously or not, went back to ideas advanced in the 1920's by Bukharin, who, in turn, tried to justify them by reference to some of Lenin's ideas. The implication is that communist policies should be free from rigid coordination by Moscow. From this, Titoism developed the idea that in foreign policy as well a communist country should pursue its own aims rather than act as a Soviet satellite. In the beginning, the assumption was that, however independent of Moscow it might be, Yugoslav foreign policy should not be directed against the USSR. The autonomists assumed a compatibility of the interests of all socialist states. Immediately after the war, many Eastern European communist leaders seem to have felt likewise; the independent foreign-policy schemes of Dimitrov in Bulgaria, or the conflicts between the German Democratic Republic, on the one hand, and Poland and Czechoslovakia, on the other, could not otherwise be explained or justified. From this, however, it is only a small step to neutralism; and both Tito and his more orthodox colleagues in other Eastern European countries have at times declared themselves uninterested in the conflict between the USSR and the Western powers. The Yugoslav communists have wavered on this. At the time of writing, they are committed to a neutralist position, sometimes referred to as "national communism." At the time of the Hungarian uprising of 1956, they supported the Soviet intervention on the ground that socialism had to be saved from counterrevolution, thus indicating that, in a pinch, they could make only one choice between Soviet domination and the abandonment of socialism.

Titoism, furthermore, turned its attention to the Soviet Union and criticized Soviet communism as a perversion or distortion of the founding father's (Lenin's) intentions. Here Tito and his followers went back to the views first expressed by Trotsky that the Russian Revolution had gone wrong by producing a top-heavy bureaucratic machine, the members of which had turned into a privileged, ex-

ploitative ruling class running the Soviet state for its own
interests and betraying the interests of the workers, Russian as well as foreign. Like Trotsky, Tito and his spokesmen explained this perversion by the fact that the revolution was victorious in a backward country which was not
ripe for socialism. At the same time, having been a faithful product of the Stalinist system himself, Tito for many
years was obviously reluctant to dwell on this theme but
was compelled to do so by the logic of the position in
which he had been placed. His reluctance becomes all the
more meaningful when we realize that some of his closest
associates later turned these same criticisms against his
own regime.

Finally, Titoism developed social-democratic tendencies, implying that in Eastern Europe socialism could be
constructed in a more democratic and more humane manner, through a regime which would give greater opportunities for meaningful participation and greater material
benefits to the people. The Yugoslav communists have extended ownership and limited managerial authority to
workers' councils and have decentralized economic planning and management. They have decollectivized agriculture and tried to raise productivity by giving incentives
and encouraging cooperative ventures. They have revised
the criminal code and written a constitution which di-
verges from the pattern of the Eastern European regimes.
Finally, they have even denied the necessity for a communist party and have changed the party's name and status.

Other Eastern European countries under communist
rule have not gone as far as Yugoslavia in repudiating the
Soviet model; but a good deal of diversity has nonetheless
developed. The ebb and flow of these changes is much too
complicated to be summarized here. But we have already
seen that the imposition of Stalinist uniformity on the
Eastern European allies created difficulties and that after
Stalin's death there was a growing trend toward allowing
room for variation of methods and institutions, as long,
at least, as the Soviet bloc could be kept intact. These

trends toward diversity were given a boost by the denunciation of Stalin which Khrushchev made in February
1956 at the Twentieth Congress of the Communist Party
of the Soviet Union. This de-Stalinization, of which the
famous speech was only the culmination, not only raised
painful ideological questions of how to explain Stalin's
excesses and how to make sure such abuses would not be
repeated; it also led to the repudiation of the great purges
of the 1930's and the rehabilitation of many men who
had been cast out then and later. The revision of both
theory and practice was further promoted by internal unrest and, in Poland, by sensational revelations of a former
police officer, J. Swiatlo. By 1956, the communist parties
of Hungary and Poland were in acute crises, as orthodox
Stalinists fought bitterly against reformers, with rank-and-
file communists as well as other citizens pressing for even
further concessions, and the military supporting the forces
of reform. In Hungary, this crisis brought to power a reformist communist, Imre Nagy, who went furthest in put-
ting the domestic interests of his regime above the impera-
tives of Soviet policy. The reforms turned into a revolt
against Soviet domination, which was crushed by Soviet
troops.

In Poland, the victory of the reformists over the conservative Stalinist faction was a lasting one. The first wave
of revolt against the old methods of government brought
with it sweeping reforms: the removal of Soviet military
advisors; a broad amnesty for political prisoners, and the
curbing of the police; the rehabilitation of civil servants
who had been dismissed; the cessation of the jamming of
Western broadcasts; limited debate in the national parliament (*Sejm*); and a curious alliance between the communist party and the Catholic Church. In the economic life
of the country, the reforms made an end of collectivization and brought some decentralization of economic planning and management. Workers' councils were given some
recognition, and the workers for a while were even given
the right to strike. In the fields of trade and craft and light
industry, private enterprise was permitted to reëstablish

itself; and the regime accepted credits granted by Western governments. In the field of culture and intellectual activities, there was a spontaneous growth of independent clubs, discussion circles, newspapers, and journals; free speech and free criticism, even of political affairs, flourished for a while; the universities were given a great deal of self-government, and in some fields thoroughly un-Marxist opinions were once again discussed; contacts with the West were established with a good deal of enthusiasm; and even the Church was readmitted to the schools for the purpose of giving religious instruction.

Since this first outburst of noncommunist activities and opinions, the party under Gomulka's leadership has steered a cautious and wavering course between the extremes of total indoctrination or control and total permissiveness. Many times the party has reimposed curbs on intellectual discussions and organizations, but these activities are still less fettered than in any other communist country. Moreover, in the battle between communist dogma and free discussion, the pendulum seems to swing further in the direction of freedom all the time, as even Marxist doctrines are being reinterpreted in very thorough fashion. In other matters as well, the Stalinist pattern of life, which never fully took hold, is still asserting itself against the urge for its complete abolition. Slow, gradual moves have been made to return centralization to the economy and to curb workers' control. The relationship between the party and the Church has at times been more problematic than in 1957. At the same time, collectivization has not been pressed on the peasantry. Free enterprise is still tolerated in trade and crafts, although perhaps only grudgingly. In local government, a good deal of autonomy still exists, and the citizens' participation has not been robbed of all meaning. Non-communist parties still have their representatives in the *Sejm,* and this national parliament is not altogether a rubber stamp. Its committees do some meaningful work; and even the right of interpellation remains. The Polish press, although more controlled by the party than in 1956, is livelier and less dogmatic than the press in any other communist country; in the universities, the social sciences are still pursuing inquiries that would be altogether impossible if the party enforced its orthodoxies. Within the party, revisionist critics may be removed from office or they may even be permitted to resign from the party, but they are not jailed or transformed into social pariahs. In fact, pluralistic tendencies are quite obvious within the party itself.

With all this, Poland has retained its place as a respected member of the socialist camp, even though within this camp she is regarded by many as a maverick. Indeed, as a result of the events of 1956, three distinct currents of doctrine and practice have developed within the communist bloc. There is a dogmatic "left" wing whose leaders are suspicious or fearful of even the slightest deviations from established (Stalinist) patterns. Against them stand "revisionist" or reformers who plead for what might be called a more liberal course in domestic as well as foreign policy. And, finally, there are those who play the role of mediators between the two extremes, supporting sometimes one, sometimes the other side. These various groups, it seems, are now present within almost every communist party and every communist government. They may represent, alternately, the faction in power or the opposition. It is therefore impossible to place any one of the communist regimes existing today clearly in one or the other of these rather vague categories. Only one thing is clear: endeavors to preserve uniformity within the communist bloc are a thing of the past. It should be realized, however, that even before Stalin's death, these endeavors had been frustrated by the success of the Chinese communists, who completed their conquest of the Chinese mainland in 1950.

The victory of the Chinese Communist Party over the regime of Chiang Kai-shek in 1949 was the culmination of revolutionary disturbances that had troubled the vast empire of China for more than a hundred years, disturbances which had been provoked by a great variety of problems much too complex to mention within the framework of this slender study. The immediate cause of the communist victory was the collapse of the Kuomintang government, which had become corrupt, ineffective, and unpopular. The communist revolution took different forms from that of Russia: large areas of China had for years been under communist rule, so that in fact two Chinese states existed side by side, each with its own government and army, at times collaborating with each other in an uneasy and suspicious coalition against the Japanese, but on the whole considering each other mortal enemies. The revolution consisted mainly in the conquest of the rapidly disintegrating Kuomintang state by the communist armies, the population of the former observing the conquest with hostility, indifference, relief, or enthusiasm.

Once in control of the vast Chinese subcontinent, the government of the newly established People's Republic of China quickly organized itself on lines similar to the Soviet state and instituted sweeping social changes designed to weaken or destroy big capitalism, both domestic and foreign, and landlord control. By these measures the regime tried to attract mass support among workers, peasants, and intellectuals, establish firm control over the economy, destroy hostile classes, emancipate the economy from foreign control and ownership, and try to rehabilitate a productive system gutted by years of occupation and war.

At the same time, some of the methods of the Chinese Communist Party were quite different from those applied in Russia. The chief difference at first was the party's attempt to collaborate with elements of the former ruling classes, thus to mitigate class warfare and to eradicate capitalism by nonviolent methods. In order to rationalize these differences, Chinese communists had to redefine the concept of the dictatorship of the proletariat and the idea of the best road toward socialism. These unorthodox innovations were, willy-nilly, tolerated even by Stalin.

By 1953, the government of Mao Tse-tung was sufficiently confident to launch its first five-year plan, which was to carry the economic transformation of the country a significant step further. While the first years of communist rule had eliminated landlords and absentee capitalists, the first five-year plan was to prepare the way for the collectivization of agriculture and the total socialization of industry and handicraft. China thus tried to copy the rapid transformations undergone by the Soviet economy, but in far less time, even though the base from which China started was infinitely more backward than the Russian economy of 1917. The Chinese leaders claimed that this faster rate of revolutionary transformation was made possible by generous Soviet aid and by the more advanced state of modern technology. By the fall of 1956, the outlines of the second five-year plan began to take shape. It was formally adopted in early 1957 and began to be implemented in 1958. Its goal was to drive the Chinese economy and society into the "Great Leap Forward" to industrialism and socialism. Production goals were set which seemed fantastically high to Western economists, and some of which did in fact prove to be unrealistic. Methods of organization and management were applied which in centralization and unyielding collectivism outstripped anything that had been undertaken by Soviet society; and the Mao regime even claimed that China might virtually skip some of the stages of development which had marked the history of the USSR. The most spectacular of these social experiments was the transformation of agriculture from an individual peasant system to a thoroughly collective system and the concomitant merger of agricultural pursuit with industrial construction. Unlike the Soviet *kolkhoz,* the Chinese commune makes not the slightest concessions to individualism or to family traditions. Instead, it is an attempt to apply the organizational form of the labor gang or the drill platoon not only to farming operations, large-scale construction work, and other primary economic pursuits but also to all possible human activities, including housing, feeding, education, and recreation. Here was the utter militarization of life in the intensity demanded for the working class in Plato's utopia. Vast masses of people organized into disciplined labor armies were deployed in building dams and other waterworks, roads, railroads, and entire industrial enterprises, so that the Chinese people seem to be building much of their new industrial base in bucket-brigade fashion, with legions of unskilled manual labor. These people's communes were to combine all administrative and economic functions; and the party therefore claimed that they were leading directly to the withering away of the state. More generally, Mao and his comrades asserted that the Great Leap Forward and the establishment of people's communes should be regarded as a direct step into communism; and one implication was that China might reach that happy stage even before the USSR.

Since the initiation of this Great Leap Forward, some parts of China's economic plans have had to be revised downward, as some of the goals turned out to be unrealistic. In addition, some of the most drastic features of communal life in the people's communes seem to have been mitigated. The Chinese economy, on the whole, is still beset with tremendous problems and inadequacies. And yet it has already become apparent that China is achieving rapid economic growth and may well be on her way to join the United States, the Soviet Union, Germany, and England as one of the world's major industrial nations, even though it will take time before the living standard of her more than six hundred million people can be raised appreciably. China is thus joining the ranks of the great powers.

There had been a good deal of speculation among Western journalists and politicians about growing friction between Moscow and Peking, some of this friction being attributed to the rapidity of economic development in China or to the methods by which it has been achieved. Projecting, perhaps, their own dread of the so-called colored races onto the Russians, many Western writers assert that the Kremlin leaders are bound to be deeply apprehensive about the growing strength of their great Asian neighbor, about a population that outnumbers the Soviet population more than three times, fearing that sooner or later this giant will have to seek room for expansion and encroach on Mongolia, Turkestan, the Maritime Provinces, or other Soviet territory. After all, many areas on the borders between Russia and China have changed hands before. Others maintain that Peking deeply resents Moscow, either because the Russians are a white nation, or because the Russian communists in past periods showed an overbearing attitude toward their Chinese comrades, or because the Chinese feel that the Russians have betrayed them or left them in the lurch several times in recent decades, or because Soviet Russian economic aid is not coming in sufficient quantity or comes with strings attached—even if the only string is a 1 per cent per annum interest charge on loans. After Stalin's death, many writers claimed that Mao had now become the world's senior communist, the leading spokesman and theoretician of the movement; and some of them see him engaged in a rivalry over the place of honor with Khrushchev.

There are indications, moreover, that the two senior communist governments are at odds over important ideological and political questions. The sweeping claims made by Peking about the Great Leap Forward have been soft-pedaled by Soviet ideologists; certain claims made by the Chinese about the virtues of the commune system and the possibility of jumping from colonial backwardness almost directly into communism are not even mentioned in Russia. Important elements of Chinese communist ideology are thus distorted or suppressed. Is this because Moscow resents any hint that the Chinese can do feats even the Russians could not do? Is it because the Soviet party bureaucrats are appalled at the very thought that Chinese methods of management might be tried in their own country? Or is it merely because the Soviet ideological system can not or will not tolerate even the slightest deviation from its own established dogmas? Are there, perhaps, still some Russian or European communists who have not yet forgiven Mao Tse-tung for coming to power in a manner that does not agree with Lenin's own prescriptions or with Stalin's narrow interpretation of them? Furthermore, there are increasing indications that Moscow and Peking do not agree on the ideological and policy lines the communist world should pursue in world affairs. The impression is that Mao and his Chinese comrades are in favor of continuing the cold war against the West in the most intense form or even of letting it get hot. Ever since 1955, when the so-called spirit of Geneva first replaced the icy hostility of the Cold War, the Kremlin has expressed the desire to seek an accommodation with the West (even though the terms it offered might not have been acceptable in the West), while the voice of Peking has manifested only unmitigated hatred, supreme contempt, and cockiness. In this connection, the Chinese party has also reversed its stand regarding Eastern European revisionism. While in 1956 they gave support to Gomulka and men who thought as he did, they have since reverted to the strictest ideological rigidity and to denunciation of all revisionist tendencies. In this, they are doubtless motivated, at least in part, by the necessity to keep revisionist tendencies within their own party in check.

As little as a year ago, most Western scholars would have maintained that, for the time being at least, the bonds of mutual interest which tied the Russian and Chinese regimes together were far stronger than the issues of controversy, even though an abundance of conflict material seemed to make an eventual clash between them very likely. Since then, the Twenty-second Congress of the CPSU, meeting in Moscow in the fall of 1961, surprised the world by revealing the open dissent between the two major communist powers. Mr. Chou En-lai, the chief Chinese delegate, conspicuously honored the remains of Stalin only shortly before the late dictator was shamefully ejected from his resting place beside Lenin. Later, the Chinese delegation heard bitter attacks made upon their country's policies and views, however indirectly they were stated; and, after a heated speech in defense of Albania, they walked out of the Congress. All this pointed up the seriousness of the rift. Undoubtedly, the bonds of friendship and mutual interest between Moscow and Peking are still strong. But the process of dissolution within the communist camp is apparently occurring faster than most observers had assumed.

II

The Challenge
of Communism

World communism is growing in strength and is confident of victory. This confidence can have a variety of consequences. It can lead to a relaxation of tension and the prevalence of the spirit of accommodation, because the leaders of Soviet Russia and China may become convinced that time is in their favor and that aggressive action may be too risky. The inferiority complex which forced them to be assertive, prestige conscious, and stubborn in all dealings with the West may be on the wane. The strong can afford to be generous. Or else the growing confidence of strength may make the communist leaders more cocky and demanding than ever before. Perhaps they will continue to follow both approaches. Not even Stalin dared to make demands in such threatening language as Khrushchev did over Suez and Berlin. But neither would Stalin have dared yield to Western resistance with so little fuss as Khrushchev did in withdrawing (at least temporarily) his Berlin ultimatum.

World communism is becoming increasingly diversified.

It includes today a variety of institutions and goals and attitudes, from the uncompromising stand of Mao Tse-Tung to the cautious maneuvering of Gomulka and the tame menshevism of Togliatti. While this may spell the growing ideological erosion of communism, it may also mean greater strength and therefore a challenge to the West.

Communism is a challenge to the West not only because it has managed to coexist with capitalism and to become a world power of major proportions but also because it succeeded in evoking enthusiasm in China and is beginning to have grass-roots support in Russia. The relief with which vast masses in China welcomed the defeat of the Kuomintang may by now have given way to regrets. The discipline of communes and construction armies may be attributable to the worst terror methods rather than to enthusiasm, even though there must be a significant portion of Chinese who are still drunk with the euphoria of revolutionary pioneering. Of such enthusiasm, which still moved many among Russia's young generation at the time of the first five-year plan, little seems to remain in the Soviet Union. Moreover, despite careful indoctrination in the history and the doctrines of the Communist Party, vast masses of the Soviet population seem to be as indifferent to matters of ideology as most Americans are. They read the writings of Lenin little more than our college youth read those of Jefferson or Hamilton; the resolutions of a party congress do not mean very much more to them than the platforms of our major parties do to us. But the Soviet population has nonetheless internalized significant portions of the socialist ethos, and the recent successes of the Soviet regime have given many people a strong incentive to be loyal, devoted, and cooperative.

Finally, communism challenges the West because it is so closely linked with the major revolution of our time—the emancipation of formerly dependent areas. Unlike many Americans, I am strongly convinced that this revolution would go on even if there were no communist movement, although communism helps to inspire some of

its leaders; one might even go so far as to argue that, had
the Russian Revolution not taken place and had the Russians not interfered so much in the affairs of world communism, the global revolution would have gone on more
rapidly and more successfully.* Yet, however independent
of communist initiative the global revolution may be, the
communist world is likely to derive greater benefit from it
than the Western powers.

For the last ten or fifteen years, the world has been
preoccupied with the cold war—Soviet Russia versus the
United States. But, as this page is being written, the cold
war is slowly becoming a phenomenon of the past. For
the cold war was possibly only as long as there was a
strict bipolarity of power in the world. Slowly but surely,
however, this bipolarity is giving way to a pluralism of
great powers. Within a decade or two (if civilization manages to survive), China, India, a united Africa, or other
great power blocs may have emerged. Moreover, the more
countries (if any) are added to the communist bloc, the
more difficult it will be to preserve cohesion and coordination in that world. Centrifugal tendencies, already quite
apparent among America's satellites, will become more
and more pronounced in the communist empire as well.

Once this has taken place, the stalemate of the cold
war is likely to yield to a more flexible politics of ma-
neuver, which may very well blur the seemingly ideological lines. Groups of communist and noncommunist powers may well ally themselves against other groups of
similar composition, just as a century after the Reformation Protestant and Catholic princes began to collaborate
in like fashion.

If the disaster of nuclear war can be averted, it is possible that the analogy with the Reformation may become
pertinent in many other ways. In Chapter 1, I called communism the puritanism of our century. We, of course,
then are the Catholics in that analogy. It is worth noting

* In saying this, I disagree sharply with R. N. Carew Hunt,
"The Importance of Doctrine," in *Problems of Communism*,
VII/2/12.

that puritans and papists not only came to collaborate in politics; in time they came to live with each other. Even though the two groups maintain their doctrinal disputes, and even though they may vote differently in presidential elections, it would be difficult to establish meaningful differences between a Catholic and a Protestant way of life. In most important aspects they have become very much alike.

Communism and capitalism will retain differences in traditions and culture, major differences, perhaps, in the social structure and the functioning of the economic system as a whole, equally major differences also in the process of decision making, which is called politics and government. And yet, the common problems shared by all nations committed to twentieth-century industrialism and all it implies will grow in scope. If they are left to grow without major disturbances, perhaps communism and capitalism will gradually cease to present a challenge to each other. Perhaps one of the major tasks of our age is to seek a modern Peace of Westphalia without having to go through the nightmare of a modern Thirty Years' War.

Obstacles in the way of such a solution are formidable, and perhaps they should be seen as the most profound of all the challenges which communism presents to the West. On pages 6 and 7, I pointed out that communism was not prepared, psychologically or doctrinally, for prolonged coexistence with the capitalist world. From this I deduced a certain persistent inability for self-orientation, a mental block hindering understanding, a tendency even toward character traits which border paranoia. We should be aware that the West was no more prepared for coexistence with communism; hence, we too are threatened with the loss of our sanity. Communism has established itself as a successful alternative to our own way of life, to our own pattern of social organization. But our deeply engrained convictions make it almost impossible for us to acknowledge the possibility of a successful alternative. The moral challenge inherent in it is too great to be faced. The existence of a rival political order so shakes our belief in the virtues of our social system that many of us repress this knowledge. The resultant neurosis takes the form of various delusions about the nature of contemporary world affairs. The principal function of these delusions is to reaffirm our shaken conviction that ours is the best of all possible worlds. Since, moreover, on the communist side, the urge to flee from reality is equally strong, as we have seen, the major powers in the contemporary world seem to face each other in a stance that might best be described as reciprocal paranoia. Two nervous, shaken, trigger-happy antagonists are facing each other with loaded weapons. Each *knows* the other will shoot first. Neither can do anything at all without increasing the other's suspicions and nervousness. Reciprocal paranoia may therefore make real its worst fears.

Communism thus threatens our sanity, and the great challenge is for us to preserve it. It also challenges us not to destroy our own way of life by the manner in which we respond. This is an extremely complicated problem which cannot be developed here. Suffice it to say that any attempt to slow down the spread of communism must be guided by imagination, empathy, generosity, and a deep commitment to democratic values, if it is to be successful. Whether the Western world can muster these qualities in its state of ideological shock remains to be seen. Moreover, to respond to the challenge may require changes in the policy orientation and management of the Western world which the nations of the West are not prepared to undertake. This leaves two alternatives: a conservative resolve to hold the line wherever it can be held, or a militant determination to stamp out all challenges by force. In a revolutionary world, the former is self-defeating, and in the age of fusion devices the latter may be suicidal. Both, moreover, are likely to help destroy constitutional democracy in the West.

Notes and References

CHAPTER 1 Introduction

(1) Communist efforts to persuade distinguish different publics, for instance, when they differentiate between "propaganda" and "agitation." For a definition of these terms, see Alfred G. Meyer, *Leninism* (Cambridge, Mass., 1957), p. 150.

(2) See Myron Rush, *The Rise of Khrushchev* (Washington, D. C., 1958), which in its entirety deals with communist language as an esoteric code of this sort.

(3) "Ideology and Power Politics: A Symposium," *Problems of Communism,* VII, No. 2, 10-35.

(4) See Harold J. Laski, *Reflections on the Revolution of Our Time* (New York, 1943), pp. 73-75; Eduard Bernstein, *Cromwell and Communism: Socialism and Democracy in the Great English Revolution* (London, 1930), pp. 26-30, and Leon Trotsky, *Whither England?* (New York, 1925), pp. 60-61 and *passim.*

CHAPTER 2 Marxist Theory

(1) Descriptions of the conditions of the working class in early capitalism abound not only in Marxist literature, beginning with Engels' *The Condition of the Working Class in England* (New York, 1958) and Marx's *Capital,* but are more familiar to us through the novels of Dickens, Victor Hugo, and others. For a more recent description of similar conditions in the United States, see Oscar Handlin, *The Uprooted* (Boston, 1951).

(2) *The Communist Manifesto* of Marx and Engels devotes a brief chapter to the utopian socialists.

(3) An interesting discussion of these elements in Marxism is provided in Vernon Venable, *Human Nature: The Marxist View* (New York, 1945). See also Alfred G. Meyer, *Marxism: The Unity of Theory and Practice* (Cambridge, Mass., 1954).

(4) The liberational elements in Marxism are brought out with greatest clarity, and with an emphasis that is controversial, in Raya Dunaevskaya, *Marxism and Freedom* (New York, 1958). See also Erich Fromm, *Marx's Concept of Man* (New York, 1961).

(5) See Meyer, *Marxism: The Unity of Theory and Practice.*

(6) This brief account cannot possibly touch upon the very real philosophic problems created by Marx's attempt to fulfill philosophy by overcoming it. For works treating the problem, see Selected Readings on Marxist economic doctrines. Nor is this the place to treat the complicated relationship between Marxism and contemporary social science, a problem which I have treated briefly in "Marxism and Social Science," *Centennial Review,* Fall 1959, pp. 423-436.

CHAPTER 3   European Marxism, 1848-1914

(1) This idea is expressed clearly in *The Communist Manifesto;* in Marx's *The Poverty of Philosophy;* and in the essay by Engels on the *History of the Communist League.*

(2) George Lichtheim, "Marxist Doctrine in Perspective," *Problems of Communism,* VII, No. 6, 34.

(3) See especially Erich Matthias, "Kautsky und der Kautskyanismus," in *Marxismusstudien,* II, 151-197; also Karl Korsch, *Die materialistische Geschichtsauffassung* (Leipzig, 1930).

CHAPTER 4   Principles of Leninism

(1) Geroid T. Robinson, *Rural Russia Under the Old Regime: A History of the Landlord-Peasant Revolution of 1917* (New York, 1949).

(2) For a more detailed presentation of my views, and for sources, see Alfred G. Meyer, *Leninism* (Cambridge, Mass., 1957), of which the present chapter is a brief abstract. A discussion of the history of the bolshevik faction is reserved for the following chapter.

(3) See Erich Goldhagen's brilliant article on "Ideology and the Transition to Communism," *Soviet Survey,* No. 28 (April-June 1959), pp. 56-63.

(4) V. I. Lenin, *Sochineniia* [Works] 2d ed., XXIII (Moscow, 1931), p. 220.

(5) For books on communism which emphasize this Machiavellian morality of expediency, see Philip Selznick, *The Organizational Weapon* (New York, 1952), and Stefan T. Possony, *A Century of Conflict* (Chicago, 1953).

(6) Concerning the origins of the theory of imperialism in the writings of Hobson, Hilferding, Luxemburg, and Bukharin, see Meyer, *Leninism,* and Paul M. Sweezy, *The Theory of Capitalist Development.*

CHAPTER 5   History of the Russian Communist Party up to the Death of Lenin

(1) In addition to the works by Radkey, Masaryk, Venturi, and Treadgold, cited in Selected Readings for Chapter 4, information about the *narodniks* is contained in Victor M. Chernov, *The Great Russian Revolution* (New Haven, 1936).

(2) Bertram D. Wolfe, *Three Who Made a Revolution* (Boston, 1955), has discussed these financial problems. They also receive attention in Leonard Schapiro's *The Communist Party of the Soviet Union* (New York, 1960).

(3) Merle Fainsod, *International Socialism and the World War* (Cambridge, Mass., 1935).

(4) See Isaac Deutscher, *The Prophet Armed: Trotsky 1921-1929* (Fair Lawn, N. J., 1954), for events leading up to 1921.

(5) For a summary of the issues over which opposition sentiment arose, see Alfred G. Meyer, *Leninism* (Cambridge, Mass., 1957), pp. 197-198, footnote. See also Deutscher, *The Prophet Armed: Trotsky 1921-1929*; and Leonard Schapiro, *The Communist Party of the Soviet Union.* Full treatment of these issues is given in Robert V. Daniels, *The Conscience of The Revolution* (Cambridge, Mass., 1960).

CHAPTER 6   Phases of Soviet Rule

(1) Sidney Heitman, *An Annotated Bibliography of Nikolai I. Bukharin's Published Works* (Fort Collins, 1958), not only lists more than five hundred items of published work from Bukharin's pen, but also a number of unpublished dissertations and other secondary works dealing with him. Heitman's own views on Bukharin are summarized in his "Between Lenin and Stalin: Nikolai Bukharin," in Leopold Labedz (ed.), *Revisionism: Essays on the History of Marxist Ideas* (New York, 1962). In addition, Julius Hecker, *Moscow Dialogues: Discussions on Red Philosophy* (London, 1933), and Raymond A. Bauer, *The New Man in Soviet Psychology* (Cambridge, Mass., 1959), present some Bukharinist ideas.

(2) *Capital* (Chicago, 1906), I, p. 784.

(3) *Ibid.*, I, p. 834.

(4) The term "surplus-alienation" is adapted from Herbert Marcuse, *Eros and Civilization* (Boston, 1956).

CHAPTER 7   The Communist International, 1919-1943

(1) On the Treaty of Brest Litovsk, see J. W. Wheeler-Bennett, *The Forgotten Peace* (New York, 1939); also Deutscher, *The Prophet Armed: Trotsky* (Fair Lawn, N. J., 1954); Alfred G. Meyer, *Leninism* (Cambridge, Mass., 1957); and Louis Fischer, *The Soviets in World Affairs: A History of the Relations between the Soviet Union and the Rest of the World, 1917-1929* (2 vols; London, 1930).

(2) On the German revolution of 1923, see Franz Borkenau, *The Communist International* (London, 1938), Chapter XIV; E. H. Carr, *A History of Soviet Russia*, Vol. IV, *The Interregnum* (New York, 1954), Chapters 7 and 9; Ruth Fischer, *Stalin and German Communism: A Study in the Origins of the State Party* (Cambridge, Mass., 1948), Chapters 13-16; and Jan Valtin, *Out of The Night* (New York, 1941).

(3) The speeches made by Maxim Litvinov in the League of Nations have been published in the English language. An authorized biography of Litvinov has been written by A. U. Pope, *Maxim Litvinov* (New York, 1943). The official line regarding communist policy in the period of the United Front is presented in George Dimitrov, *The United Front* (New York, 1938). For critical discussions, see Borkenau, *The Communist International*, Chapter XXII; and, by the same author, *European Communism* (New York, 1953), Chapter V.

(4) Communist activity during the Spanish Civil War has been treated in David Cattell, *Soviet Diplomacy and the Spanish Civil War* (Berkeley, Calif., 1957); George Orwell, *Homage to Catalonia* (Boston, 1955); Franz Borkenau, *The Spanish Cockpit* (London, 1937). For French politics at the time of the Popular Front policy, see Alexander Werth, *France in Ferment* (New York, 1935); and J. Danos and M. Gibelin, *Juin 36: masses et militants* (Paris, 1952). Also Franz Borkenau, *European Communism* (New York, 1953), Chapters V-VIII; Mario Einaudi *et al.*, *Communism in Western Europe* (Ithaca, N. Y., 1951); and Hugh Seton-Watson, *From Lenin to Malenkov* (New York, 1953).

(5) The effects of the Great Purge on foreign communist parties is described in Borkenau, *European Communism*, Chapters VII-VIII, and in such eyewitness accounts as Margarete Buber-Neumann, *Under Two Dictators* (London, 1949). See also Alfred Burmeister, *Dissolution and Aftermath of the Comintern* (mimeographed; New York, 1955).

(6) The techniques of setting up so-called front organizations is de-

scribed in many books dealing with communism, especially Stephen T. Possony, *A Century of Conflict* (Chicago, 1953), and Philip Selznick, *The Organizational Weapon* (New York, 1952). It is emphasized particularly in the confessional literature of former American communists, such as Louis Budenz, *The Techniques of Communism* (Chicago, 1954); Whittaker Chambers, *Witness* (New York, 1952); Benjamin Gitlow, *I Confess* (New York, 1940); and Herbert A. Philbrick, *I Led Three Lives* (New York, 1952). See also Max Kampelman, *The Communist Party versus the CIO* (New York, 1957).

(7) A classic account of communist policies between August 1939 and July 1941 is A. Rossi, *Les Communistes français pendant la drôle de guerre* (Paris, 1951) and *A Communist Party in Action* (New Haven, 1949). For speculations and analyses of Soviet motives in concluding the pact with Germany, see David Dallin, *Soviet Russia's Foreign Policy, 1939-42* (New Haven, 1942); R. J. Sontag and J. S. Beddie, *Nazi-Soviet Relations* (New York, 1948); Gustav Hilger and Alfred G. Meyer, *The Incompatible Allies* (New York, 1953); G. Weinberg, *Germany and the Soviet Union* (New York, 1954); and A. Rossi, *The Russo-German Alliance* (London, 1950).

(8) No special treatment has yet been given to the activities of communist parties during the time the USSR was involved in the second World War. Occasional remarks only can be found in much of the literature cited in the preceding notes, especially Borkenau, *European Communism*. It is regrettable that this important book is so unreliable because of its author's propensity for speculation and for citing anonymous references.

(9) On the dissolution of the Comintern, see the study by Burmeister cited in Note 5.

CHAPTER 8   The Soviet Union Describes Itself

(1) "Cadres decide everything" was said by Stalin in May of 1935. See "Struktura otdela rukovodiashchikh partiinykh organov Ts. K. partii," *Partiinoe Stroitel'stvo*, No. 17 (1935), pp. 73-78.

(2) Khrushchev's pronouncements on the incipient transition to communism are analyzed in Erich Goldhagen, "Ideology and Transition to Communism," *Soviet Survey*, No. 28 (April-June 1959), pp. 56-63. The new platform ("Program") of the CPSU, adopted in the fall of 1961, which summarizes current Soviet thinking about the impending transition to communism, can be found in numerous documentary collections, e.g., Arthur P. Mendel (ed.), *Essential Works of Marxism* (New York, 1961); or Dan N. Jacobs (ed.), *The New Communist Manifesto* (Evanston, Ill., 1962). For speculations by Western scholars on these developments, see W. Z. Laqueur and L. Labeds (eds.), *The Future of Communist Society* (New York, 1962).

(3) For a convincing attempt to decipher the esoteric code of communication used by the Soviet elite, see Myron Rush, *The Rise of Khrushchev* (Washington, D. C., 1958).

CHAPTER 9   The Soviet Way of Life

(1) For descriptions of the life of party members, see Raymond A. Bauer, Alex Inkeles, and Clyde K. M. Kluckhohn, *How The Soviet System Works* (Cambridge, Mass., 1956); Raymond A. Bauer, *Nine Soviet Portraits* (New York, 1955); and Raymond A. Bauer and Alex Inkeles, *The Soviet Citizen* (Cambridge, Mass., 1959).

(2) For works on the Soviet government see Selected Readings for Chapter 7.

(3) An interesting theory incorporating the selective enforcement of conflicting standards in Soviet administration is developed by Andrew Gunder Frank, "The Organization of Economic Activity in the Soviet Union," *Weltwirtschaftliches Archiv*, Vol. 78, No. 1 (1957), pp. 104-156.

(4) Merle Fainsod, *How Russia Is Ruled* (Cambridge, Mass., 1953), sees the Soviet political system almost entirely as an instrument of control, neglecting the many other functions performed by its governmental institutions and processes. For a view of the Soviet system as the purest specimen of a new species of government, called totalitarianism, see Bertram D. Wolfe, *Communist Totalitarianism* (Boston, 1961).

(5) This idea is expressed most sharply in Isaac Deutscher, *Russia, What Next?* (Fair Lawn, N. J., 1953). It is evaluated critically in Barrington Moore, Jr., *Terror and Progress, USSR* (Cambridge, Mass., 1954). See also Bauer and Inkeles, *The Soviet Citizen;* Alfred G. Meyer, "Russia After Stalin," *Current History,* January 1956, pp. 1-7, and Marshall D. Shulman, "Changing Appreciation of the Soviet Problem," *World Politics,* July 1958.

(6) The relationship between the Soviet government and the peasantry is summarized in Herbert Dinerstein, *Communism and the Russian Peasant* (Chicago, 1955).

(7) The recent census of the Soviet population, now in the process of being evaluated, will reveal the staggering losses in Soviet manpower during the war. For figures on Soviet losses through capture or defection in the early weeks of the war any detailed military history of the war should do. On this and on the entire story of German occupation policies, see Alexander Dallin's exhaustive study, *German Rule in Russia* (New York, 1957).

(8) Soviet wartime policies are summarized ably in Nicholas S. Timasheff, *The Great Retreat* (New York, 1946).

(9) A deluge of highly speculative and specious articles still continues to deal with the power struggles in the Kremlin following Stalin's death. One of the few convincing studies is Myron Rush, *The Rise of Khrushchev* (Washington, D. C., 1958). See also Leonard Shapiro, *The Communist Party of the Soviet Union* (New York, 1960) and Wolfgang Leonhard, *The Kremlin Since Stalin* (New York, 1962).

(10) See Selected Readings on resistance and revisionism.

(11) A convenient survey of policies pursued since 1953, and the various measures of relaxation included in them, is provided by Abraham Brumberg (ed.), *Russia Under Khrushchev* (New York, 1961).

CHAPTER 10 World Communism since World War II

(1) See Chapter 7, Note 8.

(2) An excellent bibliography of works dealing with Soviet strategic thinking is provided in chapter IX of Alvin Z. Rubinstein (ed.), *The Foreign Policy of the Soviet Union* (New York, 1960).

(3) Zbigniew K. Brzezinski, *The Soviet Bloc* (Cambridge, Mass., 1960).

(4) See Selected Readings on the Soviet image of the West.

Selected Readings

CHAPTER 1 Introduction

A sample of the more important studies we have of communism will show the wide range of approaches to the subject. There are historical studies that stress personalities or politics, such as Bertram D. Wolfe, *Three Who Made A Revolution* (Boston, 1955), and Isaac Deutscher, *Stalin: A Political Biography* (Fair Lawn, N. J., 1949), and those that focus on the history of ideas, such as Arthur Rosenberg, *A History of Bolshevism from Marx to the First Five Years' Plan* (London, 1934), and Leopold Haimson, *Russian Marxists and the Origins of Bolshevism* (Cambridge, Mass., 1955). There are works in which historical developments become almost incidental to the structure of ideas, such as Waldemar Gurian, *Bolshevism: Theory and Practice* (New York, 1932), and Alfred G. Meyer, *Leninism* (Cambridge, Mass., 1957). Theory itself has been treated in terms of its own evolution from Marxism, as in Meyer, *Leninism*, and Herbert Marcuse, *Soviet Marxism* (New York, 1958). But in other studies theory is reduced to a set of strategic devices, for example, in Philip Selznick, *The Organizational Weapon* (New York, 1952), or Nathan Leites, *A Study of Bolshevism* (Chicago, 1953). In the latter work, these strategic devices are explained, to some extent, by a presumed Russian national character. The range of approaches widens considerably when we survey works that deal with non-Russian forms of communism. We shall do that at appropriate places.

CHAPTER 2 Marxist Theory

Source Material and Secondary Works

For handy bibliographies to the vast source material and secondary works on Marxism, see John Plamenatz, *German Marxism and Russian Communism* (New York, 1954); H. B. Mayo, *Democracy and Marxism* (Fair Lawn, N. J., 1955); Robert Tucker, *Philosophy and Myth in Karl Marx* (Cambridge University Press, 1961); George Lichtheim, *Marxism* (New York, 1961).

Iring Fetscher, *Von Marx zur Sowjetideologie* (Frankfurt, 1957); Alfred G. Meyer, *Marxism: The Unity of Theory and Practice* (Cambridge, Mass., 1954); H. Arvon, *Le Marxisme* (Paris, 1955); Karl Korsch,

Karl Marx (London, 1938); Jean-Yves Calvez, S.J., *La Pensée de Karl Marx* (Paris, 1957); M. Rubel, *Bibliographie des oeuvres de Karl Marx* (Paris, 1956); and Gerhard Lehmbruch, *Kleiner Wegweiser zum Studium der Sowjetideologie* (Bonn, 1958).

Marxist Economic Doctrines

The best summary of Marxist economic doctrines is to be found in Paul Sweezy, *The Theory of Capitalist Development* (New York, 1956). See also Henry Bartoli, *La Doctrine économique et sociale de Karl Marx* (Paris, 1950); Joan Robinson, *An Essay on Marxian Economics* (New York, 1952); Joseph Schumpeter, *Capitalism, Socialism and Democracy* (3d ed.; New York, 1950); and Maurice Dobb, *Political Economy and Capitalism* (New York, 1957).

Religious Criticism of Marxism

Marxism is discussed as a secular religion in Waldemar Gurian, *Bolshevism; Introduction to Soviet Communism* (Notre Dame, Ind., 1953). Similar ideas are expressed in Gustav Wetter, S.J., *Dialectical Materialism* (New York, 1959), and in J. Hommes, *Der technische Eros* (Freiburg, 1955). For further bibliography of religious critics of Marxism, see Chapter XIV of G. Lehmbruch, *Kleiner Wegweiser zum Studium der Sowjetideologie.*

Philosophic Problems of Marxism

See Herbert Marcuse, *Reason and Revolution: Hegel and the Rise of Social Theory* (New York, 1955); Gustav Wetter, *Dialectical Materialism* (New York, 1959); Sidney Hook, *From Hegel to Marx* (New York, 1950); Karl Korsch, *Marxismus und Philosophie* (Leipzig, 1923); Georg Lukacs, *Geschichte und Klassenbewusstsein* (Berlin, 1923); Max Raphael, *Zur Erkenntnistheorie der kontreten Dialektik* (Paris, 1934); and the extensive bibliography in Iring Fetscher, "Der Marxismus im Spiegel der französischen Philosophie," *Marxismusstudien*, I, 173-213.

CHAPTER 3 European Marxism, 1848-1914

History of the Labor Movement, 1848-1890

On the history of the labor movement between 1848 and 1890, see, among others, Paul Louis, *Histoire du socialisme en France* (Paris, 1946); G. D. H. Cole, *British Working Class Politics, 1832-1914* (London, 1941); G. D. H. Cole, *A History of Socialist Thought*, Vols. II and III (New York, Vol. II 1954, Vol. III 1956); Max Beer, *A History of British Socialism* (London, 1940); Alexander Gray, *The Socialist Tradition* (New York, 1946); Arthur Rosenberg, *Democracy and Socialism* (New York, 1939); J. Lenz, *The Rise and Fall of the Second International* (New York, 1932); James Joll, *The Second International: 1889-1914* (New York, 1955); George Lichtheim, *Marxism* (New York, 1961).

Writings of Marx and Engels

The more important writings of Marx and Engels dealing with the analysis of current political events are: Karl Marx, *The Class Struggles in*

France; Karl Marx, *The Civil War in France;* Karl Marx, *The Eighteenth Brumaire of Louis Bonaparte;* Friedrich Engels, *Germany—Revolution and Counterrevolution.*

In addition to current analyses of political events, Marx and Engels ventured into history and anthropology (*The German Peasant War; The Origins of the Family, Private Property, and the State*). Marx undertook his major task of working out his analysis and critique of the capitalist economic system; *Capital,* never completed, is only the last of several attempts to accomplish this. Both he and Engels wrote on party politics and strategy, the most famous instance being his *Critique of the Gotha Program.* Finally, Engels made fragmentary attempts to extend the theory into such fields as philosophy and biology: *Ludwig Feuerbach and the Outcome of Classical German Philosophy; Herr Eugen Dühring's Revolution in Science;* and the articles collected in a posthumous volume called *The Dialectics of Nature.*

CHAPTER 4   Principles of Leninism

History of Russia

For bibliographies on the history of Russia, see Robert J. Kerner, *Slavic Europe: A Selected Bibliography* (Cambridge, Mass., 1918); Charles Morley, *Guide to Research in Russian History* (Syracuse, N. Y., 1951); and Philip Grierson, *Books on Soviet Russia* (London, 1943). General introductions to Russian history include V. O. Klyuchevsky, *A History of Russia* (5 vols.; London, 1911-1931); B. H. Sumner, *A Short History of Russia* (New York, 1949); Valentin Gitermann, *Geschichte Russlands* (Zürich, 1944-49); Karl Stählin, *Geschichte Russlands von den Anfängen bis zur Gegenwart,* 4 vols. (Berlin, 1923-39); Hans von Eckhardt, *Russia* (New York, 1932); Paul Milyukov, *Outlines of Russian Culture* (Philadelphia, 1942); P. I. Lyashchenko, *History of the National Economy of Russia to the 1917 Revolution* (New York, 1949); J. Mavor, *An Economic History of Russia* (2 vols.; London, 1914); Michael Karpovich, *Imperial Russia, 1801-1917* (New York, 1932); A. Kornilov, *Modern Russian History* (New York, 1916-1917); Sir John Maynard, *Russia in Flux* (New York, 1948); Bernard Pares, *The Fall of the Russian Monarchy: A History of Evidence* (London, 1939); Alfred Levin, *The Second Duma: A Study of the Social-Democratic Party and the Russian Constitutional Experiment* (New Haven, 1940).

Russia's Revolutionary Movements

On Russia's revolutionary movements, see Richard Hare, *Pioneers of Russian Social Thought* (Fair Lawn, N. J., 1951); J. F. Hecker, *Russian Sociology* (New York, 1915); Oliver Radkey, *The Agrarian Foes of Bolshevism* (New York, 1958); Donald Treadgold, *Lenin and His Rivals* (New York, 1955); Thomas G. Masaryk, *The Spirit of Russia* (New York, 1955); Franco Venturi, *Il Populismo Russo* (Torino, 1952); Leopold Haimson, *Russian Marxists and the Origins of Bolshevism* (Cambridge, Mass., 1955); P. Scheibert, *Von Bakunin zu Lenin* (Leiden, 1956); Nikolai Berdyaev, *The Origin of Bolshevism* (Naperville, Ill., 1955); George Fischer, *Russian Liberalism before the Revolution: From Gentry to Intelligentsia* (Cambridge, Mass., 1958); Avrahm Yarmolinsky, *Road to Revolution* (London, 1957).

CHAPTER 5 History of the Russian Communist Party up to the Death of Lenin

History of the Russian Marxist Movement

Scholarly work on the history of the Russian Marxist movement is now coming out at an increasing rate both in the USSR and the Western World. The most recent is Leonard Schapiro, *The Communist Party of The Soviet Union* (New York, 1960). Previous works include Fedor Dan, *Proiskhozhdenie Bol'shevizma* (New York, 1946); Arthur Rosenberg, *A History of Bolshevism from Marx to the First Five Years' Plan* (London, 1934); Isaac Deutscher, *Stalin: A Political Biography* (Fair Lawn, N. J., 1949), *The Prophet Armed: Trotsky* (Fair Lawn, N. J., 1954) and *The Prophet Unarmed* (New York, 1959), Bertram D. Wolfe, *Three Who Made a Revolution* (Boston, 1955); and Boris Souvarine, *Staline* (Paris, 1935). The most convenient guide to the recent rash of Soviet writings is probably provided by the journal *Voprosy Istorii KPSS*.

The Russian Revolution

Classic works on the Russian Revolution are Leon Trotsky, *The History of the Russian Revolution* (Ann Arbor, Mich., 1957); Victor M. Chernov, *The Great Russian Revolution* (New Haven, 1936); N. N. Sukhanov, *The Russian Revolution, 1917* (abridged from *Zapiski o revoliutsii*) (Fair Lawn, N. J., 1955); the first three volumes of E. H. Carr, *A History of Soviet Russia* (4 vols.; New York, 1950-1954); John Reed, *Ten Days That Shook the World* (New York, 1919). See also William Henry Chamberlin, *The Russian Revolution, 1917-1921* (2 vols., rev. ed.; New York, 1952); James Bunyan and H. H. Fisher (eds.), *The Bolshevik Revolution, 1917-1918; Documents and Materials* (Stanford, Calif., 1934); Leonard Schapiro, *The Origin of the Communist Autocracy: Political Opposition in the Soviet State: First Phase, 1917-1922* (Cambridge, Mass., 1955); and Oskar Anweiler, *Die Rätebewegung in Russland, 1905-1921* (Leiden, 1958).

The Civil War

On the civil war, see the works of Chamberlin, Schapiro, and Carr, cited above; also N. Kritsman, *Geroicheskii period velikoi Russkoi revoliutsii* (Moscow, 1924); Richard Pipes, *The Formation of the Soviet Union: Communism and Nationalism, 1917-1923* (Cambridge, Mass., 1954); John S. Reshetar, Jr., *The Ukrainian Revolution, 1917-1920* (Princeton, N. J., 1952); Firuz Kazemzadeh, *The Struggle for Transcaucasia, 1917-1921* (New York, 1951); James Bunyan (ed.), *Intervention, Civil War and Communism in Russia: April-December, 1918* (Baltimore, 1936). This list could be extended greatly. There is in addition an avalanche of documentary material, memoirs, and secondary accounts published in the USSR in recent years.

CHAPTER 6   Phases of Soviet Rule

The Period of War Communism

For descriptions of the Soviet regime in the period of war communism, see the works on the civil war cited in Selected Readings for Chapter 5. On cultural trends, consult Rene Fülöp-Miller, *The Mind and Face of Bolshevism* (New York, 1928); D. S. Mirsky, *Contemporary Russian Literature* (Fair Lawn, N. J., 1925); Nicholas Hans and Sergius Hessen, *Educational Policy in Soviet Russia* (London, 1930); and especially N. S. Timasheff, *The Great Retreat* (New York, 1946).

The Trotsky Opposition

On the Trotsky opposition, see Deutscher, *The Prophet Unarmed* (New York, 1959); Souvarine, *Staline* (Paris, 1935); Ruth Fischer, *Stalin and German Communism: A Study in the Origins of the State Party* (Cambridge, Mass., 1948); R. V. Daniels, *The Conscience of The Revolution* (Cambridge, Mass., 1960); and Alexander Erlich, *The Soviet Industrialization Debate, 1924-1928* (Cambridge, Mass., 1960).

The Industrialization Period

For literature on the industrialization period, see W. H. Chamberlin, *Russia's Iron Age* (Boston, 1934); Maurice Hindus, *The Great Offensive* (London, 1933); John Scott, *Behind the Urals* (Boston, 1942) all of them useful eyewitness accounts.

The Collective Farm System

On the collective farm system, see Lazar Volin, *A Survey of Soviet Russian Agriculture* (Washington, D. C., 1951); David Mitrany, *Marx against the Peasant* (Chapel Hill, N. C., 1952); Fedor Belov, *A History of a Soviet Collective Farm* (New York, 1956); Naum Jasny, *The Socialized Agriculture of the USSR* (Stanford, Calif., 1949); Herbert Dinerstein, *Communism and the Russian Peasant* (Chicago, 1955); and Roy D. Laird, *Collective Farming in Russia*.

The Great Purge, the Secret Police, and Labor Camps

On the Great Purge and the secret police, the literature is of tremendous bulk. An attempt to explain police terror as a functional aspect of the Soviet social system is made in Zbigniew K. Brzezinski, *The Permanent Purge: Politics in Soviet Totalitarianism* (Cambridge, Mass., 1956). A large number of conflicting explanations of the Great Purge are offered in F. Beck and W. Godin, *Russian Purge and the Extraction of Confession* (New York, 1951). See also Alex Weissberg, *The Accused* (New York, 1951); Nathan Leites and Elsa Bernaut, *Ritual of Liquidation* (Chicago, 1954); on the police system, Simon Wolin and Robert M. Slusser (eds.), *The Soviet Secret Police* (New York, 1957); on labor camps, David J. Dallin and Boris I. Nicolaevsky, *Forced Labor in Soviet Russia* (New Haven, 1947); also numerous eyewitness accounts such as Jerzy Gliksman, *Tell The West* (New York, 1948). There are a number of fictionalized treatments of the Great Purge; outstanding among them is Arthur Koestler, *Darkness at Noon* (New York, 1956).

The Cultural Counterrevolution

See Nicholas S. Timasheff, *The Great Retreat* (New York, 1946); Kurt London, *The Seven Soviet Arts* (London, 1937); Klaus Mehnert, *Stalin versus Marx* (London, 1952); Harold J. Berman, *Justice in Russia* (Cambridge, Mass., 1950); Raymond A. Bauer, *The New Man in Soviet Psychology* (Cambridge, Mass., 1959); Herbert Marcuse, *Soviet Marxism* (New York, 1958). A wealth of additional suggestions can be found in the chapters on philosophy, religion, social relations, science, literature, music, and other arts in the valuable bibliographic book, H. H. Fisher (ed.), *American Research on Russia* (Bloomington, Ind., 1959).

The Transformation of Marxism

On the transformation of Marxism, see the works by Marcuse, Mehnert, and Bauer cited above. See also Gustav Wetter, S.J., *Dialectical Materialism* (New York, 1959); I. Bocheński, *Der sowjetrussische dialektische Materialismus (Diamat)* (Bern, 1950); Max Gustav Lange, *Marxismus-Leninismus-Stalinismus* (Stuttgart, 1955); Henri Chambre, S.J., *Le Marxisme en Union Soviétique* (Paris, 1955); and the extensive bibliographies in the works by Wetter and Bocheński.

CHAPTER 7   The Communist International, 1919-1943

The Communist International

Useful introductions to the history of the Communist International are provided by Hugh Seton-Watson, *From Lenin to Malenkov* (New York, 1953); Franz Borkenau, *The Communist International* (London, 1938); G. D. H. Cole, *Communism and Social-Democracy, 1914-1931* (London, 1959); Stefan T. Possony, *A Century of Conflict* (Chicago, 1953); Arthur Rosenberg, *A History of Bolshevism from Marx to the First Five Years' Plan* (London, 1934); and Ossip K. Flechtheim, "Die Internationale des Kommunismus 1917-1957," *Zeitschrift für Politik*, VI (Neue Folge), No. 3, 231-252. For documentary collections, see Olga Gankin and H. H. Fisher (eds.), *The Bolsheviks and the World War* (Stanford, Calif., 1940); Robert V. Daniels, *A Documentary History of Communism* (New York, 1960); and Jane Degras, *The Communist International* (Fair Lawn, N. J., 1956). See also E. H. Carr, *A History of Soviet Russia*, Vol. I, *The Bolshevik Revolution* (New York, 1950); Robert V. Daniels, *A Documentary History of Communism* (New York, 1961); and Ruth Fischer, *Stalin and German Communism: A Study in the Origins of the State Party* (Cambridge, Mass., 1948); Ossip K. Flechtheim, *Die KPD in der Weimarer Republik* (Offenbach am Main, 1948); Leon Trotsky, *The First Five Years of the Communist International* (New York, 1945); Theodore Draper, *The Roots of American Communism* (New York, 1957); I. Howe and L. Coser, *The American Communist Party* (Boston, 1958); C. H. Sévène, *Les origines du communisme en France* (Paris, 1953); Gérard Walter, *Histoire du Parti Communiste Français* (Paris,

1948); and Michael T. Florinsky, *World Revolution and the USSR* (New York, 1933).

Soviet Foreign Relations

An excellent introduction to the history of Soviet behavior in the world arena is provided by Alvin Z. Rubinstein, *The Foreign Policy of the Soviet Union* (New York, 1960).

On Soviet foreign policy in Europe before World War II, see Louis Fischer, *The Soviets in World Affairs: A History of the Relations between the Soviet Union and the Rest of the World, 1917-1929* (2 vols.; London, 1930); Max Beloff, *The Foreign Policy of Soviet Russia* (Fair Lawn, N. J., 1947-1949); Mario Einaudi *et al.*, *Communism in Western Europe* (Ithaca, N. Y., 1951); G. Hilger and Alfred G. Meyer, *The Incompatible Allies* (New York, 1953).

On Soviet policy in Asia up to World War II, see the pertinent sections in the works cited above on the Communist International; also Allan Whiting, *Soviet Policies in China, 1917-1924* (New York, 1954); Benjamin I. Schwartz, *Chinese Communism and the Rise of Mao* (Cambridge, Mass., 1951); Xenia Eudin and Robert C. North (eds.), *Soviet Russia and the East, 1920-1927* (Stanford, Calif., 1957); Conrad Brandt, *Stalin's Failure in China: 1924-1927* (Cambridge, Mass., 1958); M. A. Kennedy, *A Short History of Communism in Asia* (London, 1957); G. D. Overstreet and Marshall Windmiller, *Communism in India* (Berkeley, Calif., 1959); M. Masani, *The Communist Party of India* (New York, 1954); John Kautsky, *Moscow and the Communist Party of India* (New York, 1956); Rodger Swearingen and Paul Langer, *Red Flag in Japan* (Cambridge, Mass., 1952); Charles MacLane, *Soviet Policy and the Chinese Communists, 1931-46* (New York, 1958); Harold Isaacs, *The Tragedy of the Chinese Revolution* (Stanford, Calif., 1951); David Dallin, *Soviet Russia and the Far East* (New Haven, 1948); Walter Z. Laqueur, *Communism and Nationalism in the Middle East* (New York, 1956); George Lenczowski, *Russia and the West in Iran* (Ithaca, N. Y., 1953); Harry Miller, *The Communist Menace in Malaya* (New York, 1954); G. Hanrahan, *The Communist Struggle in Malaya* (New York, 1954); Malcolm D. Kennedy, *A History of Communism in East Asia* (New York, 1957).

On the alliance with the Kuomintang and other features of Soviet-Chinese relations, see the brilliant book by Alan Whiting, *Soviet Policies in China, 1917-1924* (New York, 1954); also Conrad Brandt, *Stalin's Failure in China* (Cambridge, Mass., 1958). For documents, see Xenia Eudin and Robert C. North, *Soviet Russia and the East, 1920-1927* (Stanford, Calif., 1957); C. M. Wilbur, *Documents on Communism, Nationalism and Soviet Advisers in China, 1918-1927* (New York, 1956); and Conrad Brandt, John Fairbank, and Benjamin Schwartz, *A Documentary History of Chinese Communism* (Cambridge, Mass., 1952).

The Rise of Mao Tse-tung

The rise of Mao Tse-tung has been treated in Benjamin I. Schwartz, *Chinese Communism and The Rise of Mao* (Cambridge, Mass., 1951). See also Robert C. North, *Moscow and the Chinese Communists* (Stanford, Calif., 1953); Kuo-chun Chao, *The Communist Movement in China; A Chronology of Major Developments* (Cambridge, Mass., 1950); Edgar Snow, *Red Star Over China* (New York, 1939); and Charles MacLane, *Soviet Policy and the Chinese Communists* (New York, 1958); also Harold Isaacs, *The Tragedy of the Chinese Revolution* (Stanford, Calif., 1951).

CHAPTER 8   The Soviet Union Describes Itself

Dialectical Materialism

English-language outlines of dialectical materialism by communist au-
thors include V. Adoratsky, *Dialectical Materialism* (New York, 1934);
Maurice Cornforth, *Science and Idealism* (New York, 1947); David A.
Guest, *Textbook of Dialectical Materialism* (New York, 1939); and
Howard Selsam, *Handbook of Philosophy* (New York, 1949); to which
we might add the sympathetic treatment in John Somerville, *Soviet
Philosophy* (New York, 1946). For critical treatment, see Gustav A.
Wetter, *Dialectical Materialism* (New York, 1959); I. M. Bocheński,
Der sowjetrussische dialektische Materialismus (*Diamat*) (Bern, 1950);
and Max Gustav Lange, *Marxismus-Leninismus-Stalinismus* (Stuttgart,
1955). For ample bibliographical information about Soviet works on the
subjects, see the work by Wetter cited above and Raymond A. Bauer,
The New Man in Soviet Psychology (Cambridge, Mass., 1959). See also
H. H. Fisher (ed.), *American Research on Russia* (Bloomington, Ind.,
1959), pp. 68-70.

CHAPTER 9   The Soviet Way of Life

History and Structure of the Communist Party

The history and structure of the Communist Party of the Soviet Union
have been treated in considerable detail in Merle Fainsod, *How Russia
Is Ruled* (Cambridge, Mass., 1953), and Julian Towster, *Political Power
in the USSR* (Fair Lawn, N. J., 1948). The party's function in a locally
restricted area is vividly portrayed in Merle Fainsod, *Smolensk under
Soviet Rule* (Cambridge, Mass., 1958). Exhaustive histories of the party
are about to appear; for the time being, we have to study it through the
use of biographies of Lenin, Trotsky, and Stalin, especially those by
Deutscher, Souvarine, and Trotsky. John A. Armstrong, *The Soviet
Bureaucratic Elite* (New York, 1959), deals with the party *aktiv* in the
Ukraine; and the title of Sidney Harcave, *The Structure and Functioning
of the Lower Party Organizations in the Soviet Union* (Maxwell Air
Force Base, Ala., 1954), explains itself. An exhaustive bibliographic
essay on Soviet sources has been published, though only in mimeographed
form, by John A. Armstrong, *An Essay on Sources for the Study of the
Communist Party of the Soviet Union, 1934-1960* (Madison, Wisconsin,
1961). See further Robert V. Daniels, "The Secretariat and the Local
Organizations in the Russian Communist Party," *American Slavic and
East European Review,* February 1957; also Louis B. Nemzer, "The
Kremlin's Professional Staff: The 'Apparatus' of the Central Committee,
Communist Party of the Soviet Union," *American Political Science Re-
view,* XLIV, No. 1 (March 1950), 64-85.

Soviet Government

Soviet government is described in Merle Fainsod, *How Russia Is Ruled*
(Cambridge, Mass., 1953); Julian Towster, *Political Power in the USSR*
(Fair Lawn, N. J., 1948); Derek Scott, *Russian Political Institutions*
(New York, 1958); Barrington Moore, Jr., *Soviet Politics* (Cambridge,

Mass., 1950), Chapters 11-12. Very brief introductions are provided by
John N. Hazard, *The Soviet System of Government* (Chicago, 1957);
John A. Armstrong, *Ideology, Politics, and Government in the Soviet
Union* (New York, 1962); and Frederick L. Schuman, *Government in
the Soviet Union* (New York, 1961). Bertram D. Wolfe, *Communist
Totalitarianism* (Boston, 1962) provides an interpretation which might
be balanced by reading Zbigniew K. Brzezinski, *Ideology and Power in
Soviet Politics* (New York, 1962), as well as the discussion on the nature
of the Soviet social system in *Slavic Review*, vol. XX, No. 3 (October
1961). For the development of soviets, see Oskar Anweiler, *Die Rätebewegung in Russland, 1905-1921* (Leiden, 1958); for local government
organization, see Merle Fainsod, *Smolensk under Soviet Rule* (Cambridge,
Mass., 1958); for electoral practices, George Barr Carson, *Electoral
Practices in the U.S.S.R.* (New York, 1956).

The Soviet Economy

Harry Schwartz, *Russia's Soviet Economy* (Englewood Cliffs, N. J.,
1954), although still useful as an introduction to the functioning of the
Soviet economy, is outdated by now. But three excellent works are now
available to serve this purpose: Alec Nove, *The Soviet Economy* (New
York, 1961); Robert W. Campbell, *Soviet Economic Power* (Cambridge,
Mass., 1960); and a symposium published by the Joint Economic Com-
mittee, Congress of the United States, *Comparisons of the United States
and Soviet Economies,* parts I-III (Washington, 1960). See also Alexander
Baykov, *The Development of the Soviet Economic System* (New York,
1946); Maurice Dobb, *Soviet Economic Development since 1917* (New
York, 1948); and Naum Jasny, *The Soviet Economy during the Plan
Era* (Stanford, Calif., 1951).

The headaches of a Soviet plant manager are described in David
Granick, *The Red Executive* (New York); Joseph S. Berliner, *Factory
and Manager in the USSR* (Cambridge, Mass., 1957); and David Granick,
Management of the Industrial Firm in the USSR (New York, 1953).
See also Alexander Vucinich, *Soviet Economic Institutions* (Stanford,
Calif., 1952); and Gregory Bienstock, Solomon M. Schwarz, and Aron
Yugow, *Management in Russian Industry and Agriculture* (London,
1944).

An interesting comment on the Soviet rat race is provided in Mark
Field, *Doctor and Patient in Soviet Russia* (Cambridge, Mass., 1957). For
a discussion of Stakhanovism and other devices for raising the productivity of labor, see Solomon M. Schwarz, *Labor in the Soviet Union*
(New York, 1951).

Rewards

See Janet G. Chapman, "Real Wages in the Soviet Union, 1928-1952,"
Review of Economics and Statistics, XXXVI, No. 2 (May 1954), 134-
156.

The rise in Soviet living standards in recent years is discussed by
Alec Nove and a number of commentators in *Problems of Communism*,
IX, No. 1, 1-22.

Regarding the growing literature on social mobility in the USSR, see
Chapter 6 of H. H. Fisher (ed.), *American Research on Russia* (Bloomington, Ind., 1959), especially 86-96.

Sanctions

An interesting interpretation of Soviet criminal law is provided in Harold J. Berman, *Justice in Russia* (Cambridge, Mass., 1950). See also John Hazard, "Trends in the Soviet Treatment of Crime," *American Sociological Review*, V, No. 4 (August 1940), 566-576, and Mark Field, "Drink and Delinquency in the USSR," in *Problems of Communism*, IV, No. 3, pp. 29-37. The interpretation of terror as "prophylactic justice" is given in Jerzy Gliksman's contribution to Carl J. Friedrich (ed.), *Totalitarianism* (Cambridge, Mass., 1954). The function of terror is analyzed in Barrington Moore, Jr., *Terror and Progress, USSR* (Cambridge, Mass., 1954); Zbigniew K. Brzezinski, *The Permanent Purge* (Cambridge, Mass., 1956); and Albert K. Herling, *The Soviet Slave Empire* (New York, 1951). Joseph Scholmer, *Vorkuta* (New York, 1955) is recent enough to relate the disturbances that broke out in some of the camps after Stalin's death. A general treatise attempting to analyze all these accounts is David J. Dallin and Boris I. Nicolaevsky, *Forced Labor in Soviet Russia* (New Haven, 1947).

On Soviet labor camps there is a wealth of literature, such as Jerzy Gliksman, *Tell The West* (New York, 1948); Elinor Lipper, *Eleven Years in Soviet Prison Camps* (Chicago, 1951); and Albert K. Herling, *The Soviet Slave Empire* (New York, 1951). Joseph Scholmer, *Vorkuta* (New York, 1955) is recent enough to relate the disturbances that broke out in some of the camps after Stalin's death. A general treatise attempting to analyze all these accounts is David J. Dallin and Boris I. Nicolaevsky, *Forced Labor in Soviet Russia* (New Haven, 1947).

For the structure of the police apparatus, see Otto Heilbrunn, *The Soviet Secret Services* (New York, 1956); and Robert Slusser and Simon Wolin, *The Soviet Secret Police* (New York, 1957). Of Soviet defectors who have described their activities under the Soviet police system, the most valuable book seems to be Peter Deriabin and Frank Gibney, *The Secret World* (New York, 1959).

Education

Literature concerning the Soviet educational system is cited in Note 13, p. 216, of H. H. Fisher (ed.), *American Research on Russia* (Bloomington, Ind., 1959). See also George Z. F. Bereday and Jaan Pennar (eds.), *The Politics of Soviet Education* (New York, 1960). Alex Inkeles, *Public Opinion in Soviet Russia: A Study in Mass Persuasion* (Cambridge, Mass., 1950), is a general treatise on the Soviet mass media of communication. See also Bruno Kalnins, *Der sowjetische Propagandastaat* (Stockholm, 1956); P. Babitsky and John Rimbarg, *The Soviet Film Industry* (New York, 1955); Merle Fainsod, "Censorship in the USSR," in *Problems of Communism*, V, No. 2, 12-19; and Leo Gruliow, "How the Soviet Newspaper Operates," *ibid.*, pp. 3-11.

National Minorities

On national minorities, see A. G. Park, *Bolshevism in Turkestan* (New York, 1957), John A. Armstrong, *Ukrainian Nationalism, 1939-1945* (New York, 1955); Basil Dmytryshyn, *Moscow and the Ukraine* (New York, 1956); John S. Reshetar, Jr., *The Ukrainian Revolution* (Princeton, N. J., 1952), Nicholas P. Vakar, *Belorussia: The Making of a Nation* (Cambridge, Mass., 1956); Firuz Kazemzadeh, *The Struggle for Transcaucasia* (New York, 1951); Richard Pipes, *The Formation of the Soviet*

Union (Cambridge, Mass., 1954); Frederick Barghoorn, *Soviet Russian Nationalism* (Fair Lawn, N. J., 1956); and the chapters dealing with national minorities in Waldemar Gurian (ed.), *Soviet Imperialism* (Notre Dame, Ind., 1953). A superficial survey reflecting the Soviet point of view is Corliss Lamont, *The Peoples of the Soviet Union* (New York, 1946).

Resistance and Revisionism

Apathy, malingering, delinquency, and other forms of escape, evasion, or rebellion are discussed in R. A. Bauer, Alex Inkeles and Clyde K. M. Kluckhohn, *How the Soviet System Works* (Cambridge, Mass., 1956); Bauer and Inkeles, *The Soviet Citizen* (Cambridge, Mass., 1956); and Bauer, *Nine Soviet Portraits* (New York, 1955). See also Mark Field, *Doctor and Patient in the Soviet Union* (Cambridge, Mass., 1957); Joseph S. Berliner, *Factory and Manager in the USSR* (Cambridge, Mass., 1957); and the bibliographical information in Chapter 6 of H. H. Fisher (ed.), *American Research on Russia* (Bloomington, Ind., 1959).

Walter Z. Laqueur and George Lichtheim (eds.), *The Soviet Cultural Scene* (New York, 1958) concentrates its attention on evidence of intellectual ferment in the USSR since the death of Stalin. See also the quarterly publication *Soviet Survey*, and Leo Labedz (ed.), *Revisionism: Essays on the History of Marxist Ideas* (New York, 1962).

The current struggle against revisionism and the growing diversity of opinions on various matters can be followed by glancing through any recent issues of Soviet learned or political journals. Important articles are usually translated into English in the *Current Digest of the Soviet Press*. Some of the more interesting controversies and opinions are printed in the (apparently Soviet-sponsored) *Soviet Review*.

CHAPTER 10   World Communism since World War II

Communism in Eastern Europe

The wartime negotiations between Soviet Russia, England, and the United States are related in such memoirs as Winston S. Churchill, *The Second World War* (Boston, 1948-1953); Robert E. Sherwood, *Roosevelt and Hopkins* (rev. ed.; New York, 1950); James F. Byrnes, *Speaking Frankly* (New York, 1947); and Edward R. Stettinius, Jr., *Roosevelt and the Russians* (New York, 1949). The case of Poland is discussed by Edward J. Rozek, *Allied Wartime Diplomacy* (New York, 1957). See the bibliography for Chapter V of Alvin Z. Rubinstein (ed.), *The Foreign Policy of the Soviet Union* (New York, 1960); and the works cited at the close of Chapter 24 of Donald W. Treadgold, *Twentieth Century Russia* (Chicago, 1959).

The most convenient introduction to the transformation of Eastern Europe into a group of communist governments remains Hugh Seton-Watson, *The East European Revolution* (London, 1950). See also R. R. Betts (ed.), *Central and South Eastern Europe* (Fair Lawn, N. J., 1950); A. Gyorgy, *Governments of Danubian Europe* (New York, 1949); J. Roucek (ed.), *Moscow's European Satellites* (Annals of the Amer. Acad. of Pol. Sci., Vol. 27, Sept. 1950); Doreen Warriner, *Revolution in Eastern Europe* (London, 1950); and Zbigniew K. Brzezinski, *The Soviet Bloc* (Cambridge, Mass., 1960). For treatments of individual countries, the list could be made very long. Among the more important works we might name Otto Friedman, *The Breakup of Czech Democracy* (London, 1950); P. Barton, *Prague à l'heure de Moscou* (Paris, 1954); P. J. Nettl, *The Eastern Zone and Soviet Policy in Germany* (Fair Lawn, N. J., 1951); Henry L. Roberts, *Rumania* (New Haven, 1951); Samuel Sharp, *White Eagle on a Red Field* (Cambridge, Mass., 1953); I. Gadourek, *Political Control of Czechoslovakia* (Leiden, 1953). For bibliographical information, see also Jirina Sztachova, *Mid-Europe; A Selective Bibliography* (New York, 1953); and C. E. Black, "The People's Democracies of Eastern Europe," in Taylor Cole (ed.), *European Political Systems* (New York, 1953).

The early hopes for Europe's "own road" to socialism are treated incidentally in many of the works cited in the foregoing footnote. See also Adam Ulam, *Titoism and the Cominform* (Cambridge, Mass., 1952); C. P. McVicker, *Titoism; Pattern for International Communism* (New York, 1957); J. Montgomery, *Hungary, The Unwilling Satellite* (New York, 1947); D. A. Tomasic, *National Communism and Soviet Strategy* (Washington, D. C., 1957).

The break with Tito is traced on the basis of the correspondence between Belgrade and Moscow in Robert Bass and Elizabeth Marbury (eds.), *The Soviet-Yugoslav Dispute* (London, 1948).

The theory and practice of Titoism is described in the works cited above. See also Robert Bass and Elizabeth Marbury (eds.), *The Soviet-Yugoslav Controversy, 1948-58: A Documentary Record* (New York, 1959); H. F. Armstrong, *Tito and Goliath* (New York, 1951); V. Dedijer, *Tito* (New York, 1953); S. Clissold, *Whirlwind: An Account of Marshal Tito's Rise to Power* (London, 1949); F. W. Neal, *Titoism in Action: Reforms in Yugoslavia, 1948-1954* (Berkeley, Calif., 1958).

For works on the Soviet domination and exploitation of Eastern Europe between 1945 and 1953, see the works cited above on the transformation of Eastern Europe; also A. Cretzianu (ed.), *Captive Rumania: A Decade of Soviet Rule, 1945-1955* (New York, 1956); C. Milosz, *The Captive Mind* (New York, 1953); Robert Slusser, *Soviet Economic Policy in Postwar Germany* (New York, 1953); D. A. Schmidt, *Anatomy of a Satellite* (Boston, 1952); W. J. Stankiewicz and J. M. Montias, *Institutional Changes in the Postwar Economy of Poland* (New York, 1955). The Cominform is treated in Franz Borkenau, *European Communism* (New York, 1953), Chapter 20, and in B. S. Morris, "The Cominform: A Five-Year Perspective," in *World Politics*, VI, 368-376.

The intellectual ferment and the revolts in Eastern Europe, 1953-1956, are the themes of the following works: Henry L. Roberts, "The Crisis in the Soviet Empire," *Foreign Affairs*, Vol. 35, pp. 191-200; Paul Zinner (ed.), *National Communism and Popular Revolt in Eastern Europe* (New York, 1956); Konrad Syrop, *Spring in October: The Polish Revolution of 1956* (London, 1957); Edmund Stillman (ed.), *Bitter Harvest* (New York, 1959); Imre Nagy, *On Communism; In Defense of the New Course* (New York, 1957); Tamas Aczel and Tibor Meray, *The Revolt of the Mind* (New York, 1959); Tibor Meray, *Thirteen Days That Shook the Kremlin* (New York, 1959).

The Cold War

The cold war is treated in every book on Russia, communism, or world affairs that has appeared since about 1948. For a special treatment, see

Kenneth Ingram, *History of the Cold War* (New York, 1955); E. D.
Carman, *Soviet Imperialism: Russia's Drive toward World Domination*
(Washington, D. C., 1950); W. P. Davison, *The Berlin Blockade* (Prince-
ton, N. J., 1958); Xenia J. Eudin, "Moscow's View of American Im-
perialism," *Russian Review*, Vol. 13, pp. 276-284; C. G. Haines (ed.),
The Threat of Soviet Imperialism (Baltimore, 1954) and Hugh Seton-
Watson, *Neither War Nor Peace* (New York, 1960). See also the ex-
tensive bibliography for Chapters 6 and 7 of Alvin Z. Rubinstein (ed.),
The Foreign Policy of the Soviet Union (New York, 1960).

Regarding the breaking of the ice (the thaw) in the cold war, see the
Columbia University publication, *The Anti-Stalinization Campaign and
International Communism* (New York, 1957); Evron M. Kirkpatrick
(ed.), *Target—The World* (New York, 1957); Bernard Morris, "Soviet
Policy toward National Communism: The Limits of Diversity," *The
American Political Science Review*, LIII, No. 1 (March 1959), 128-137;
Harry Schwartz, *The Red Phoenix* (New York, 1961); and Wolfgang
Leonhard, *The Kremlin Since Stalin* (New York, 1962).

The Soviet Image of the West

For systematic expositions of the Soviet image of the West, the reader
will have to consult Soviet sources dealing with recent world history.
American speculations about Soviet images, thoughts, and motives are
presented in a convenient anthology in Alexander Dallin (ed.), *Soviet
Conduct in World Affairs* (New York, 1960). Some selected pronounce-
ments by Lenin, Stalin, and Khrushchev have been printed in Robert A.
Goldwin and Marvin Zetterbaum (eds.), *Readings in Russian Foreign
Policy* (2d ed., 3 vols.; Chicago, 1953). A more ample selection is pro-
vided in Alvin Z. Rubinstein (ed.), *The Foreign Policy of the Soviet
Union* (New York, 1960).

Communist Parties of the Western World

On the communist parties of the Western world, see Gabriel Almond,
The Appeals of Communism (Princeton, N. J., 1954); Philip Selznik, *The
Organizational Weapon* (New York, 1952); Hadley Cantril, *The Politics
of Despair* (New York, 1958); Wilson Record, *The Negro and the
Communist Party* (Chapel Hill, N. C., 1951); John Gates, *The Story of
an American Communist* (New York, 1958); Robert J. Alexander, *Com-
munism in Latin America* (New Brunswick, N. J., 1957); Franz Borkenau,
European Communism (New York, 1953); Mario Einaudi *et al.*, *Com-
munism in Western Europe* (Ithaca, N. Y., 1951); Morris L. Ernst and
David Loth, *Report on the American Communist* (New York, 1952);
Max M. Kampelman, *The Communist Party versus the CIO* (New York,
1957); William A. Nolan, *Communism versus the Negro* (Chicago, 1951);
James Oneal and G. A. Werner, *American Communism* (New York,
1947); I. Howe and L. Coser, *The American Communist Party* (Boston,
1958); G. Walter, *Histoire du Parti Communiste Français* (Paris, 1948).
Very ample bibliographical information on the communist parties of
France and Italy is provided in the work by Einaudi and others cited
here.

Communism and the Colonial Revolution

Works dealing with the relationship between communism and the
colonial revolution are cited at the end of Chapters X and XI of Rubinstein (ed.), *The Foreign Policy of the Soviet Union* (New York, 1960).

Communism in China

On the causes and development of the Chinese Revolution, see, among others, Charles Patrick Fitzgerald, *Revolution in China* (New York, 1952); M. N. Roy, *Revolution and Counterrevolution in China* (Calcutta, 1946); and John K. Fairbank, *The United States and China* (Cambridge, Mass., 1958).

On the first few years of communist government in China, see Otto Van der Sprenkel, Michael Lindsay, and Robert Guillain, *New China: Three Views* (London, 1950); Peter S. H. Tang, *Communist China Today* (New York, 1958); Walt W. Rostow *et al., Prospects of Communist China* (New York, 1954); Frank Moraes, *Report on Mao's China* (New York, 1953); Derk Bodde, *Peking Diary* (New York, 1950); Richard Walker, *China Under Communism* (New Haven, 1955); H. A. Steiner, *Chinese Communists in Action* (Los Angeles, 1953); N. Y. Gluckstein, *Report on Mao's China* (Boston, 1957). The Chinese five-year plan is described in the more recent of these books, especially those by Tang and Gluckstein. For information about the Great Leap Forward, we shall have to await systematic treatment.

Chinese ideological developments are discussed in the contribution of Benjamin I. Schwartz to Howard L. Boorman *et al., The Moscow-Peking Axis: Strengths and Strains* (New York, 1957). See also Z. K. Brzezinski, *The Soviet Bloc* (Cambridge, Mass., 1960), Chapter 6.

For a discussion of causes for friction between Moscow and Peking, as well as factors of cohesion, see H. Boorman *et al., The Moscow-Peking Axis: Strengths and Strains* (New York, 1957).

An annotated bibliography of English-language works on Chinese communism, together with a guide to more ambitious bibliographic works, is provided by Allan B. Cole, *Forty Years of Chinese Communism: Selected Readings with Commentary* (Service Center for Teachers of History, Publication No. 47, Washington, 1962).

Index